People Smart.
In Business

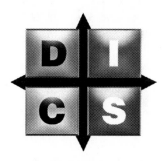

Using the DISC Behavioral Styles Model
to Turn Every Business Encounter
into a Mutual Win

Tony Alessandra, Ph.D.
and
Michael J. O'Connor, Ph.D.
with Janice Van Dyke, Ph.D.

PLATINUM RULE PRESS
Morgan James Publishing • NEW YORK

People Smart:
In Business

ISBN: 1-933596-61-9 (Paperback)

Published by:

✚ PLATINUM RULE PRESS

Morgan James Publishing, LLC
1225 Franklin Ave Ste 32
Garden City, NY 11530-1693
Toll Free 800-485-4943
www.MorganJamesPublishing.com

Cover/Interior Design by:
Rachel Campbell
rcampbell77@cox.net

Habitat
for Humanity®
Peninsula
Building Partner

"Alessandra and O'Connor have hit a real home run with *People Smart*. It's the best thing I've ever seen written in this area! It is a must read for anyone who wants to learn more about themselves and others—easy to read, but powerful in content. *People Smart* will make you more aware and more effective from the moment you finish reading it."

Kenneth Blanchard, Ph.D.

Co-author, *The One Minute Manager*

Dedications

From Tony Alessandra:

To my children, Justin & Jessica Alessandra

To my stepchildren, Ashley & Dana Wexler

From Michael O'Connor:

To Mary Ann, my loving wife and my greatest teacher, and to my children Kevin and Kara, for their patience, tolerance, and appreciation of my life's work

Acknowledgments

Writing this book has become more and more a team effort as we have progressed from one stage to the next. Some people contributed content, either directly or indirectly; others gave helpful comments about the manuscript; some recharged our batteries when the going got rough; and some reached seemingly unreachable deadlines to keep the project going on time.

With this in mind, the authors would like to thank Carl Jung, David Merrill, Larry Wilson, Performax, Dr. John Geier, William Moulton Marston, and Myers and Briggs for their pioneering research and observations.

Those who gave valuable feedback on the manuscript include Rick Barrera, Sheila Murray-Bethel, Don Cipriano, Judy Zitzloff, Marcia Feener, Charles Boyd and Jay Lewis.

Many others contributed input on their particular behavioral types-- Ron Friedman, Holli Catchpole, Paula Cathcart, Danny Colleran, John Lee, Catherine Carpenter, Stan Leopard, Mikala Limbrecht Rahn, Seymour Myers, and Jessica and Justin Alessandra.

A very special thanks to Gary Alessandra for his tireless dedication in getting several days of copy ready "yesterday", Linda Brown and Lynda London for transforming text into graphics and for making the format "reader friendly." Dee Jones and Catherine Carpenter made sure everything was organized and sent off to the right people at the right time.

Table of Contents

Introduction

Behavioral differences are our boon and our bane. They're what makes life so rich and fascinating and often so frustrating, too. Especially in our personal lives, where effective interpersonal communication with our friends, family and loved ones is pivotal.

Most of us never figure people out. We just ricochet through life. We get along great with some people, refuse to deal with others, or have as little interaction as possible with still others, because they are so different from us.

However, what if you knew the secret of those differences? What if there was a simple, but proven, way to build rapport with everyone? To eliminate interpersonal conflicts? To take charge of your own compatibility with others? To make our interactions with friends, family and loved ones mutually beneficial instead of a contest of wills?

You literally hold such a key in your hands. A product of psychological research and practical application, People Smart is a proven method of connecting with anyone in the workplace and is indispensable to anyone who is curious about what makes themselves and others tick.

You can learn to handle people the way those people want to be handled and to speak to them in the way they are comfortable listening.

People watching

We want this book to be readable, practical, and accurate. What's more, we want you to be able to remember the principles of People Smart easily. Therefore, we are using a simple, four-style model that spans all cultures and has been validated with hundreds of thousands of people, the

DISCstyles model. It focuses on patterns of observable, external clues that will give you a sense of what's going on inside someone else's head. Once you know that, you can decide how best to respond.

Everybody is interested in finding out more about themselves—and how to deal with others more effectively. If you're like most people, you want to improve your interactions with others. This book shows you a simple, yet proven, way to positively influence others.

The purpose of *People Smart* is threefold:

- Understand your own style, its strengths and weaknesses, and how your behaviors communicate that style to others.

- Identify someone else's style by quick, easily learned techniques so you will know how to "read people" and treat them the way they would like to be treated.

- Adjust your behavior to make all kinds of people more at ease with you, and you with them!

People Smart will not only help you become a better you, it will help you behave more maturely and productively by teaching you how to focus on your goals instead of your fears. Then you can develop and use more of your natural strengths, while recognizing, improving upon, and modifying your weaknesses. This book does not deal with values or judgments. Instead, it concentrates on individuals' needs and fears—our natural tendencies that cause us to do the things we do.

This book will teach you to become a people-watcher extraordinaire, someone who really understands behavioral differences and can use them to mutual advantage. This can often spell the difference between success and failure.

Every person has his or her own special way of doing things and an identifiable and predictable behavioral type. Behavioral type is a pattern, or group of recurring habits, resulting from the way you typically do things—the way you deal with people and situations. It's your comfortable method of behaving, most of the time, when you relax and just *act yourself.*

Often, when we do what comes naturally we alienate others without realizing it. Why? Because that same behavior may not be natural for them. If we want to get along with our friends, family and loved ones, it's essential we become aware of our natural tendencies—and their natural preferences! Then we can defuse extreme behaviors before we sabotage ourselves. We do this by temporarily using behavioral modification to change only our own behavior so the other person feels comfortable. When this happens, tension lessens and cooperation zooms.

Your technique of interacting with people succeeds when you receive and heed their external signals; it fails when you ignore and cross them. Of course, everyone experiences the same basic human needs, but each of us ranks some needs higher than others.

When you understand something about your own habitual style and how it differs from others' styles, you can modify your approach to get on the same wavelength with them. The ideas you present don't change. But you can change the way you present those ideas. And people will teach you how to treat them if you're willing to discover their unique signals.

For example, one type of person measures his success by results. They head for the finished product and the bottom line. They'll do whatever it takes, within reason, to get the job done. In fact, their natural response to what they view as other people's lack of accomplishment is, "Don't just sit around wasting time! Get busy!" They need achievements.

Another type places high value on recognition and measures success by the amount of acknowledgment and praise they receive.

Consequently, they typically follow that route to attention and applause. They gravitate toward friendliness and enjoyment, popularity and prestige—while consciously avoiding rejection, negativism, and arguments.

Then we have the steady, cooperative type of person who needs close relationships. They place a high value on sharing and trust, but bases their feelings about people and things on concrete evidence. They want the security and predictability found in daily routine—so they resist sudden, unplanned changes and need stable, predictable environments. They thrive on the familiar. Changes or surprises make them uncomfortable.

The last type is concerned more with content than with congratulations. They want to know how things work so they can evaluate how correctly they function. At the extreme, this tendency toward perfectionism can result in *paralysis by analysis*. Because they need to be right, they prefer checking processes themself. Concerned with appearances, they focuses on the process—how to perform a task—while complying with established rules and regulations. As the most cerebral of the four types (in terms of how they deal with people and situations, not I.Q.), tasks win over people and a slow pace prevails.

Infinite uses

The uses of People Smart are infinite. This book will show you how to build bridges to each style in any interpersonal situation.

In fact, People Smart will likely change your relationships forever. You will see people differently, understand them better, and be able to deal with them in a way that can turn every encounter into a win-win situation.

In addition, perhaps for the first time, you will truly understand your own behavior and why you act the way you do. You will see how to round off your own sharp edges and to develop strengths you did not know you had.

Some people reject the notion of "types" or "styles." Putting people in boxes, they say, is not the way to really get to know one another. Instead, they contend, that's stereotyping, a process that may be unfair to the individual and uses unrealistic shortcuts to appreciating unique human beings.

Understanding someone's behavioral style is not mutually exclusive with genuinely getting to know them. Far from it. In fact, using People Smart can greatly accelerate that process. If you can quickly notice another person's needs-based cues and adapt your own behavior, you will learn to value others more genuinely. You will see that their needs are just as valid as yours are, and you can, if you choose, seek to meet those desires and forge a deeper relationship.

Not manipulation

Another important point: When we talk about using People Smart, we are not talking about manipulating people! Rather, we are talking about learning, in a way, to speak their language.

It is not considered manipulative to speak French when in Paris, for example. Au contraire. It's something you do briefly while on the Frenchman's soil so you can be more compatible. You do not alter your basic nature while in France. Your ideas do not change. However, how you present those ideas does change.

Similarly, practicing People Smart does not fundamentally change you or the other person. It empowers you by making you multilingual, in a sense. Knowing how to listen and speak in the "language" of those around you is a delightful, useful tool that can be used to resolve differences, maximize strengths, and enjoy a fuller, more successful life by better understanding yourself and the people around you.

This is a reader-friendly book, with lots of charts and graphs to summarize and explain the text. The reader can use and reuse it as a constant companion for dealing with difficult people and stressful situations. *People Smart* shows clearly how to understand both your own unique strengths and inherent shortcomings and those of others. It gives you the tools to get what you want in various life situations with family, friends and loved ones. This book equips you with the power and knowledge to cash in on its insights through more positive and productive exchanges with others. You can realistically take charge of improving all your relationships and this book shows how.

Chapter 1
The Platinum Rule

Personality clash or instant rapport?

In your dealings with others, have you ever experienced a personality conflict? (If you haven't, check to see if you're still breathing like the rest of us mortals). No matter how much you may try, your teeth clench and your adrenaline pumps faster when you're with this difficult character. Whatever you may want to call the process, you clash. You're not tuned in on the same wavelength.

When we clash with someone, we often move towards the extreme of avoiding that person, no matter what. Or the other extreme of telling him exactly what we think of his unacceptable behavior. Or we may tell everyone else how distasteful we find him. Or just grit our teeth and tolerate him. Whatever our initial reaction, we feel uncomfortable because we have a personality conflict.

On the other hand, we'll bet you can think of somebody you liked immediately. You had instant rapport, immediate chemistry. "Ann is so down-to-earth, I feel as though I've known her for years." After ten minutes you felt like you'd known Mr. or Ms. Wonderful for half a lifetime. Here was a soul mate who clicked with you from word one. Her personality "felt right" and you also felt good about yourself when you were near her. You felt relaxed and comfortable with this person. Chemistry prevailed, and Ann made your Top Ten list of favorites.

What could possibly account for these two extreme variations in the human species? Certainly, our unique sets of experiences coupled with the genes passed down by Mom and Dad ensure we're all different. Everyone's idea of a person to avoid versus a best friend varies. Given these subjective differences, the way people communicate can result in conflict or chemistry. So how do you go about interacting with all those fascinatingly diverse, sometimes difficult, people out there?

How to deal with difficult people

This book will teach you how to treat people in a way that allows them to feel comfortable with you, so there'll be less tension between you. When tension goes down, positive outcomes---trust, credibility, creativity, cooperation, respect, commitment, and productivity--go up. How do you get results with people? By communicating with them on their level so they're at ease. Because challenging relationships are a fact of life, we'd like to show you how to:

- Understand your own style, its strengths and weaknesses, and how your behaviors communicate that style to others.

- Identify someone else's style by quick, easily learned techniques so you'll know how to "read people" and treat them the way they'd like to be treated.

- Adjust your behavior to make all kinds of people more at ease with you, and you with them!

Bending the Golden Rule

We contend that you can create much more chemistry and far less conflict in all your relationships--work, social, dating, and family--

based on how well you practice the Golden Rule. If you exercise the Golden Rule appropriately, you'll create much more relationship chemistry. But if you fail to understand the true spirit of the Golden Rule, you'll create many more personality conflicts. Just to make sure you have the proper perspective, what is the Golden Rule?

It's simply, "Do unto others as you would have them do unto you." Not the managerial version--"The person with the gold makes the rules,"--or the skeptical interpretation--"Do unto others before they do unto you."

"So," you say? "How could people get in trouble if they practiced that truth? Living by the Golden Rule should result in more harmonious relationships, not create conflict!" You're right. The problem lies with practicing the Golden Rule verbatim and not understanding its true intent. When you misapply it, you stand a much greater chance of triggering conflict over chemistry.

Let's explain. When you treat others as you want to be treated, you can end up offending others who have different needs, wants, and expectations from you. So when you apply the Golden Rule verbatim, there's a much greater chance of triggering conflict over chemistry. Yes, you heard it right? If you literally apply, "Do unto others as you would have them do unto you," you'll make problems for yourself with up to 75% of the types of people you meet. Following the Golden Rule verbatim means treating others from your point of view. That means you naturally tend to speak in the way you are most comfortable listening; or sell to others the way you like to be sold; or manage the way you want others to direct you.

When you treat people as you seek to be treated, it can cause tension. Why? Because the other person may not like your way. Perhaps you fill your own needs instead of his or hers. Or speak in a way that's easy for you to follow, but hard for the other person. That brings us to the second reason the Golden Rule can actually damage relationships. It implies all people want to be treated the same when, in fact, our preferences are not all alike. So application of this principle varies from one individual to the next based on their personality differences.

Linda treats you as she wants to be treated

The Golden Rule would work only in a perfect world where all of us were identical. But we're not. For instance, Linda devoutly practices it, but it backfires. She treats everybody alike. The world population is part of her extended Italian family.

Linda is an exceptionally people-oriented, outgoing person. She's so gregarious, when she goes to a restaurant, she greets the hostess and other patrons as though they're in her kitchen. Anyone who makes eye contact with her is fair game.

As she approaches a table of complete strangers, she typically says, "Hello? My name is Linda. What's yours? She joins in other people's conversations. She doesn't mind being asked personal questions. Readily and willingly misapplying the Golden Rule, she asks other people personal questions--whether they want to answer or not. "What is the special occasion?" Or, "What do you do for a living?"

If we take a poll at that restaurant, half the people will probably think that Linda is wonderful, but the rest of them are likely to react or think differently. As well meaning and people-oriented as she is, she often unintentionally steps on people's toes. She doesn't want to, but. . .

What has happened? Linda puts the Golden Rule into action and, by doing so, impresses some people and depresses others. Well, maybe she doesn't exactly depress them, but heightens their tensions. By acting the way she likes to be treated, there are mixed reviews. When behaving from only her own perspective, she doesn't take others' preferences into account. Why not? Simply because it's okay if strangers approach her and ask about her intimate, private thoughts; so she naturally figures it's okay for her to do the same thing. It's true for the rest of us. If we don't think first of the other person, we run the risk of unintentionally imposing a tension-filled "win/lose" or "lose/lose" relationship on them.

The Platinum Rule

We believe in refining The Golden Rule to take into consideration the feelings of the other person. Notice, we don't say break the rule. We redefine it into the Platinum Rule--"Do unto others as they want to be done unto." Treat others the way they want to be treated. By "platinum," we don't mean to imply "better." We simply want to capture the true spirit or actual intention of the Golden Rule so we consider and respond appropriately to the other person's needs. We can learn to treat different people differently, according to their needs, not ours. That leads to greater understanding and acceptance.

Remember the famous TV show, "All in the Family?"

"Edith do you know why we can't communicate? Because I'm talking in English and you're listening in dingbat!" Well, maybe Archie Bunker could benefit from learning how to communicate in "dingbat"! Then, he could mentally change places with Edith to understand her expectations instead of just his own.

Every day we face the potential for conflict or success with different types of people. Conflicts are inevitable, but the outcome from how you handle dissension is much more controllable. At the very least, you can manage your end of it. You can choose to treat somebody from his perspective, the way he wants to be treated by modifying your own behavior; or you can choose to meet only your own needs--facing consequences such as dissatisfaction, frustration, confusion, and distress. It's up to you.

Modify your spots

"Modify my behavior? Hey, I don't want to change! And I hate phonies!"

We're not talking about changing a leopard into an elephant. We mean acting in a sensible, successful way. When someone wants to move at a faster pace, move at that pace. If others want more facts and details, provide them.

But wait? Isn't it phony to act in a way that isn't natural for you? We think acting in a way that is responsive to Japanese behavior patterns in a Japanese environment is more likely to be appreciated and accepted there. The result is greater success! It helps dispel the stereotype that has been associated with some tourists who "act themselves" and expect others to do likewise. Of course, anything that's new feels strange at first, until you get more comfortable with it through repeated practice.

People learn to become more adaptable through education, experience, and maturity. We simply have to allow the opportunity for appropriate behaviors to surface. As we've mentioned, if you're able to put yourself in the other person's position, you become more open-minded in dealing with him or her. When you understand the way the other person feels comfortable communicating, you can modify your approach to get on the same wavelength. You haven't changed your own natural personality. You've merely added to it still other consciously learned, behavioral insights and strengths for dealing with different types of people and situations. The best part is that people will teach you how to communicate with them if you're willing to learn their signals by "reading" and then appropriately responding to them.

Background of behavioral types

People have been both frustrated and fascinated with each other's differences for thousands of years. The earliest recorded efforts to explain our differences were made by astrologers who recorded the positions of the heavens. The twelve signs in four basic groupings--Earth, Air, Fire, and Water--are still used today.

In ancient Greece, Hippocrates' concept of four temperaments followed---Sanguine, Phlegmatic, Melancholy, and Choleric. He viewed personality as shaped by blood, phlegm, black bile, and yellow bile. As unpalatable as this might sound to us, people accepted these physical or bodily causes for varying "humours" for centuries. Respected figures from medical/physical sciences, metaphysics, mathematics, and philosophy observed these four temperaments--including Aristotle, Empedocles, Theophrastus, and, in Roman times, Galen. References to Hippocrates' Big Four can be found in Shakespeare's plays.

In 1923, Dr. Carl Jung wrote his famous Psychological Types, at that time the most sophisticated scientific work on personality. In it, he again described four behavioral styles--the Intuitor, Thinker, Feeler, and Sensor.

This basic, four-type model spans all cultures? East and West, north and south. For instance, Japanese people still study behavior and physical composition. Advice on How to Form a Good Combination of Blood Types, a former best seller by Toshitaka Nomi, claimed 100,000 documented cases of cross-referencing personalities with blood types. Nomi indicated that 40 percent of Japan's population has Type A blood. He associated this with the conscientious, hard-working behavior expected of engineers and technicians. He hypothesized that this explained Japan's emphasis on high-technology excellence.

Four styles with a difference

Today's Information Age features more than a dozen varied models of our behavioral differences. But they all have one common thread-- the grouping of behavior into four categories.

Most of these explanations of behavioral styles have focused on internal characteristics leading to external behaviors. People Smart focuses on patterns of observable, external behaviors that each style shows to the rest of the world. It also demystifies those lesser known, but scientifically proven, internal forces which are the motivating clues behind our behaviors. In other words, this book will help you understand why you do what you do. Because we can see and hear these external behaviors, that makes it much easier for us to "read" people. Therefore, our model is simple, practical, easy to remember and use, and extremely accurate.

Our model divides people into four natural, core behavioral types:

The Dominant Director

The Interacting Socializer

The Steady Relater

The Cautious Thinker

So. . .which are you?

Chapter 2

I Know Who You Are, But What Am I?

S o how do you identify your behavioral type? Here's how! You begin by choosing those traits that most and least describe you from a list of one-word possibilities. At first, you might think, "All these sound like me," or "None of them do," but select your personal traits from these commonly found choices with a clear focus in mind. Your reward will be in arriving at one behavioral type that is more descriptive of you than any of the others.

Any of us occasionally may behave like each of the four types, but we behave in predominantly one style more of the time. The most familiar place where you operate most comfortably is called your core behavioral type--your own unique personality style. This is most evident when you just "act yourself." This natural tendency appears when you don't think about how to act. It's where you're found when your mind is on automatic pilot. This type of core behavior is your home base. To discover your behavioral type, go to http://www.platinumrule.com

PERSONAL ASSETS INVENTORY *

INSTRUCTIONS FOR RESPONDING & SCORING

A. In the space below, identify those behaviors that have typically been

Most-to-Least characteristic of you. Working left to right, assign "4" points to the MOST characteristic, "3" to the next most characteristic, then "2" and finally "1" to your least characteristic behavior.

EXAMPLE

<u>3</u> DIRECTING

<u>4</u> INFLUENCING

<u>1</u> STEADY

<u>2</u> CAUTIOUS

B. Total the numbers in each of the **four** columns. Place the **total** number for each column in the **blank** at the bottom of the column.

C. When **all four** columns are **added** together, they must equal 50.

COLUMN 1	COLUMN 2	COLUMN 3	COLUMN 4
4 Directing	3 Influencing	2 Steady	1 Cautious
4 Decisive	3 Optimistic	2 Patient	1 Restrained
2 Daring	3 Enthusiastic	1 Stabilizing	4 Analytical
4 Competitive	1 Talkative	2 Accommodating	3 Precise
4 Forceful	3 Charming	1 Easygoing	2 Curious
18 TOTAL	13 TOTAL	8 TOTAL	11 TOTAL

HOW TO DETERMINE YOUR "CORE" STYLE

If your highest column TOTAL is under column 1, you are a **Dominant Director**.

If your highest column TOTAL is under column 2, you are an **Interacting Socializer**.

If your highest column TOTAL is under column 3, you are a **Steady Relater**.

If your highest column TOTAL is under column 4, you are a **Cautious Thinker**.

This personal inventory is a simple measure of your actual behaviors. Think of your personal traits across the variety of environments and periods of your life. Complete this inventory as you see yourself. To do this, start asking yourself, "Is this or isn't this really me? If you want to take the full 30 question online assessment with a personalized 29-page report, visit http://www.DISCstyles.com/assessmentorder.asp

Look at the overall results to determine which of the four behavioral patterns you see as the single MOST and LEAST characteristic of you. Also, notice the specific behaviors within the inventory that you may have identified as MOST or LEAST characteristic of you. Later, you may want to use the same instrument to help you reevaluate your own and others' pattern(s) in four major settings—work, social, family, and romance.

An overview of the four types

THE DOMINANT DIRECTOR:

Look at my accomplishments!

Goals and Fears

Dominant Directors, driven by the inner need to lead and be in personal control, take charge of people and situations so they can reach their goals. Since their key need is achieving, they seek no-nonsense, bottom line results. Their motto is: "Lead, follow, or get out of the way." They want to win, so they may challenge people or rules. Similarly, Dominant Directors also accept challenges, take authority, and go head first into solving problems. Closely related to Dominant Directors' goals are their fears: falling into a routine, being taken advantage of, and looking "soft". So they may go to extremes to prevent those fears from materializing. They may act impatient, but they make things happen.

"Do as I say"

Since Dominant Directors need to have control, they like to take the lead in both business and social settings. They sometimes behave almost claustrophobically if they perceive someone is trying to stymie them. As natural renegades, Dominant Directors want to satisfy their need for autonomy. They want things done their way or no way at all.

Strengths and weaknesses

They often prefer strong directive management and operational tendencies and work quickly and impressively by themselves. Dominant Directors try to shape their environments to overcome obstacles en route to their accomplishments. They demand maximum freedom to manage themselves and others, using their leadership skills to become winners. Additionally, Dominant Directors often have good administration and delegation skills. This matches their motivating need. In fact, if they could delegate their exercise regimens or visits to the dentist's office, they probably would.

These assertive types tend to appear cool, independent, and competitive. They opt for measurable results, including their own personal worth, as determined by individual track records. Of all the types, they like and initiate changes the most. We symbolize this personality type with a lion--a leader, an authority. At least, they may, at least, have the inner desires to be #1, the star, or the chief.

Less positive Dominant Director components include stubbornness, impatience, and toughness. Naturally preferring to take control of others, they may have a low tolerance for the feelings, attitudes, and "inadequacies" of co-workers, subordinates, friends, families, and romantic interests.

From general to specific

Dominant Directors process data conceptually by using deductive reasoning--from general to specific information. They are more comfortable using the left brain more than the right. When combined with their need for control, this helps us better understand the emphasis on getting down to the bottom line results.

Masters of "mind control"

They may use various "mind control" techniques to help them focus on one task priority at a time. For instance, some are adept at blocking out distractions when they immerse themselves in projects. They don't hear voices, sirens, or doorbells. They seem to channel all their energies into specific jobs. Similarly, in a summer biology class, the instructor, Dr. Rains, seemed oblivious to the smell (and the grumbling) when his students dissected decomposed fish. While the class choked and hurried from their desks to the windows to gulp for air, Dr. Rains instructed them like the odor were an everyday occurrence. No big deal. Not to him, anyway.

Venting relieves their tension

Under pressure, Dominant Directors are likely to rid themselves of anger by ranting, raving, or challenging others. They naturally react to tense situations with a fight response. This tendency reflects the Dominant Directors' natural blind spots concerning other people's views and feelings. Although this venting allows the relief of their own inner tensions and hostilities, other personality types may feel intimidated by this natural, (for them!) stress reducing practice. But the Dominant Directors' barks usually exceed their bites, and they may soon forget what specifically upset them in the first place.

"Watch this performance"

Dominant Director musicians and performers typically seek to simultaneously command the stage and awe their audience. They envision themselves rising above their admirers and peers and moving into the position of number one, the best ever. Vince Lombardi, the former coach of the Green Bay Packers, coined this typical Dominant Director statement: "Winning isn't everything; it's the only thing."

Dominant Director Territory

Two cultures which have produced many Dominant Directors are northern, industrialized Germany and South Africa. These examples are not meant to over-generalize or stereotype individual behavior; instead, they help us understand how cultures tend to socialize or group people into patterns of behavior which are more consistent with past customs and expectations. In this regard, it's easier for us to understand the more natural Dominant Director behaviors. These have emerged as the expected norms or preferred behavioral patterns over the long, colorful histories of both Germany and South Africa. How often have you described people you know of German or South African background by the following behavioral descriptions of the Dominant Director temperament mentioned throughout this chapter?

- take charge--naturally seek control; want to run things their way
- controlling--fear losing personal power or status
- competitive--want to win
- motivated to be #1--seek being first or "on top" whether other people approve or not
- task-focused--strive to get the job done; often less aware of others' feelings--which may make them appear insensitive
- "no nonsense"--view life in terms of overcoming the obstacles to their successful achievement of desired results
- strong-willed--once they make up their minds, preferring to stick to their ideas; even becoming headstrong, especially under stress
- impatient--expect other people to help them get results, ASAP!!!
- fast-paced--often somewhat involved with many projects simultaneously; may even exhibit "workaholism" tendencies

Action Plan...
DOMINANT DIRECTOR
CHARACTERISTICS

SO YOU ...

Concerned with being #1	— Show them how to win, new opportunities
Think logically	— Display reasoning
Want facts and highlights	— Provide concise data
Strive for results	— Agree on goal and boundaries, then support or get out of their way
Like Personal Choices	— Allow them to "do their thing," within limits
Like changes	— Vary routine
Prefer to delegate	— Look for opportunities to modify their work load focus
Want others to notice	— Compliment them on accomplishments what they've done
Need to be in charge	— Let them take the lead, when appropriate, but give them parameters
Tendency towards conflict	— If necessary, argue with conviction on points of disagreement, backed up with facts; don't argue on "personality" basis

THE INTERACTING SOCIALIZER:

Hey, look at me!

Outgoing, Supporting, Interacting Socializers

He-e-e-ere's the Interacting Socializer!--the person who likes to go where the action is. Typically, he is outwardly energetic or fast-paced, and relationships tend to naturally take priority over tasks. The Interacting Socializer tries to influence others in an optimistic, friendly way focused on positive outcomes, whether in the social or work environment. In other words, if he shows others he likes them, he figures others will be more likely to reciprocate by responding favorably towards him. Since recognition and approval motivate him, he often moves in and around the limelight and hub of activity.

Goals and Fears

He wants your admiration and thrives on acknowledgment, compliments, and applause. "It's not just whether you win or lose. . .it's how you look when you play the game." People's admiration and acceptance typically mean more to this type than to any other. If you don't talk about him, he may spend considerable time talking about his favorite subject--himself--to gain the acceptance he wants. His biggest fear is public humiliation--whether appearing uninvolved, unattractive, unsuccessful, or unacceptable to others. These frightening forms of social rejection threaten the Interacting Socializer's core need for approval. Consequently, he may go to extremes to avoid public humiliation, lack of inclusion, or loss of social recognition.

Strengths and weaknesses

Interacting Socializers' primary strengths are their enthusiasm, persuasiveness, and friendliness. They are idea people who have the ability to get others caught up in their dreams. With great persuasion, they influence others and shape their environments by building alliances to accomplish results. Then they seek nods and comments of approval and recognition for those results. If compliments don't come, Interacting Socializers may invent their own. "Well, Harry, I just feel like patting myself on the back today for a job well done!" They are stimulating, talkative, and communicative. This type can be represented by a porpoise--playful, sociable, and talkative.

Their natural weaknesses are too much involvement, impatience, being alone, and short attention spans. This causes them to become easily bored. When a little data comes in, Interacting Socializers tend to make sweeping generalizations. They may not check everything out, assuming someone else will do it or procrastinating because redoing something just isn't exciting enough. When Interacting Socializers feel they don't have enough stimulation and involvement, they get bored and look for something new again. . .and again. . .and again. When taken to an extreme, their behaviors can be seen as superficial, haphazard, erratic, and overly emotional.

"Let me entertain you!"

If they pursue the entertainment field for careers, Interacting Socializers typically allow their natural, animated emotions to show and flow. They become stimulated by the movement and reactions of the audience, trying to get the audience to figuratively fall in love with them by acting charming and friendly. They want viewers to feel, "He (or she) is fabulous!"

Two countries brimming with Interacting Socializers

Every country, culture, and sub-culture socialize their society's members into typical daily patterns of behavior. In this respect, both Ireland and Italy are often mentioned as settings where this Interacting Socializer type seems quite commonplace. Globally, people refer to them as highly emotional people who tend to "wear their hearts on their sleeves." The Irish are known for their animated, interactive storytelling and neighborhood socializing. In fact, many areas of the Northeastern United States have become settled as Irish-Italian communities by these immigrants with similar lifestyles.

Italians' Interacting Socializer attributes have made them world-famous in the performing arts, restaurant and hospitality fields, and other person-to-person areas such as fashion and sales. How often have you described a native Irishman or Italian you have met by the following general description of the Interacting Socializer tendencies?

- optimistic--prefer to view life's positives; often block out negative situations, facts, concerns

- fast-paced--talk, move, and do most activities rather quickly

- emotional--readily show their own feelings and respond to others' feelings

- approval-seeking--look to others for acceptance and re-energizing; want people to approve of and like each other, too

- fun-loving--seek an upbeat, positive, casual atmosphere and love a good party, especially with friends

- excitable--show emotions and become enthusiastic, at best; rattled, at worst--when pressured or tired

- spontaneous--behave impulsively; dislike planning or dealing with follow-through details

- expressive--at times, they may forget and divulge secret information; or they may say too much to the wrong people

Action Plan...

INTERACTING SOCIALIZER CHARACTERISTICS

INTERACTING SOCIALIZER CHARACTERISTICS	SO YOU . . .
Concerned with approval and appearances	— Show them that you admire and like them
Seek enthusiastic people and situations	— Behave optimistically and provide upbeat setting
Think emotionally	— Support their feelings
Want to know the general expectations	— Avoid involved details, focus on the "big picture"
Need Involvement and people contact	— Interact and participate with them
Like changes and innovations	— Vary the routine; avoid repetition
Want others to notice THEM	— Compliment them personally and often
Often need help getting organized	— Do it together
Look for action and stimulation	— Keep up a fast, lively pace
Want feedback that they "look good"	— Mention their accompiish-ments, progress and your other genuine appreciation

THE STEADY RELATER:

Notice how well liked I am

Goals and fears

This type, as sung by Aretha Franklin in her hit record, may privately want a little "R-E-S-P-E-C-T", as demonstrated by your sincere personal attention and acceptance of them. Steadiness and follow-through actions characterize these people. They prefer a slower and easier pace: "It's not whether you win or lose. . .it's the friendship that counts." They focus on building trust and getting acquainted because they aim for long-standing personal relationships. Pushy, aggressive behavior secretly irritates them.

Steady Relaters strive for security. Their goal is to maintain the stability they prefer in a more constant environment. To Steady Relaters, while the unknown may be an intriguing concept, they prefer to stick with what they already know and have experienced. "Risk" is an ugly word to Steady Relaters. They favor more measured actions, like keeping things as they have been and are, even if the present situation happens to be unpleasant. Related to their goal of keeping things very similar is their accompanying fear of change and disorganization. Consequently, any disruption in their routine patterns can cause distress in Steady Relaters. Fearing sudden changes, they are naturally concerned with what may happen. A general worry is that the unknown may be even more unpleasant than the present. They need to think and plan for changes. Finding the elements of sameness within those changes can help minimize their stress by identifying the specific assurances required to cope with such demands.

Strengths and weaknesses

Steady Relaters naturally "wear well" and are an easy type to get along with. They prefer stable relationships which don't jeopardize anyone, especially themselves. Steady Relaters can be represented by the ko-ala with its accompanying slower, steady pace; relaxed disposition; and appearance of approachability and warmth. Steady Relaters have a tendency to plan and follow through. This helps them to routinely plug along. But they have their own type of unique difficulties with speaking up, seeming to go along with others or conditions, while inwardly, they may or may not agree. More assertive types might take advantage of this Steady Relater tendency to give in and avoid con-frontation. Additionally, Steady Relaters' reluctance to express them-selves can result in hurt feelings. But if Steady Relaters don't explain their feelings, others may never know. Their lack of assertiveness can take a toll on their health.

Take it slow

Steady Relaters yearn for more tranquility and security in their lives than the other three types. They often act pleasant and cooperative, but seldom incorporate emotional extremes such as rage and euphoria in their behavioral repertoire. Unlike Interacting Socializers, Steady Re-laters usually experience less dramatic or frequently occurring peaks and valleys to their more moderate emotional state. This reflects their natural need for composure, stability, and balance.

"Just plain folks"

Picture Edith Bunker of the classic sitcom ALL IN THE FAMILY. She lends a tone of continuity, coziness, and "motherliness" to virtu-ally every scene in which she appears. Edith mothers everyone around her. With her easygoing manner, she projects a genuine liking and ac-ceptance of her family, friends, and acquaintances. She's a comfortable person to watch and listen to who emanates that "I'm just a regular person" modesty. She puts on no airs and projects contentment with present conditions--just as they are and always have been.

"May I entertain you?"

In the same respect, Steady Relater celebrities tend to give predictable deliveries. Both the audience and performer may seem to merge because the Steady Relater feels so in tempo with his or her viewers. Typical audience responses may include: "He's truly one of us!" Or, "It's like being with a member of the family or my closest friend!" Steady Relaters welcome group participation, and their performances reflect their natural give and take.

Two countries with many Steady Relaters

Two Steady Relater countries that seem to have emphasized this lifestyle as a cultural norm resulting in a disproportionate number of such individual styles, are Poland and Spain. Both cultures have historically found ways to get along with foreign elements while methodically plodding forward in the direction expected, even though that direction has often been dictated by others in the short run. The Polish people are world famous for their friendly, hard-working perseverance despite the obstacles which may confront them. And, the Spanish people (those beloved Latins) make others feel at home while practicing such distinctive customs as their renowned midday siestas. Taking siestas actually allows them to go home to their families during the workday. This is consistent with the preferred slower lifestyle of this temperament, without disrupting the differing customs of guests in their homeland.

Citizens of both countries are known in their native lands and in the United States for their neighborhood restaurants and extensive group social activities. Compare the following distinguishing characteristics of this Steady Relater type which describe people you know who've been influenced directly by their own ethnic, social group, or cultural roots:

• easygoing--calm, measured, low-key behavior and outlook

- slower paced--wait until they know the steps or guidelines before acting, then move forward in a pre-set manner

- patient-- define themselves by their desire for stable relationships with others; often view problems or concerns as workable

- predictable--favor routine and stable conditions and practices

- persevering--likely to stick to a project for longer periods of time or at least until the concrete results have been produced

- modest--less likely to "blow their own horns", but are appreciative when others acknowledge their contributions

- accommodating--like to get along with others through predictable role relationships

- neighborly--prefer friendly, pleasant, helpful working relationships

Action Plan...

STEADY RELATER

CHARACTERISTICS	SO YOU …
Concerned with stability	— Show how your idea minimizes risk
Think logically	— Show your reasoning
Want documentation	— Provide facts and proof
Like personal involvement	— Demonstrate your interest in them
Need to know two-step-by-step sequence	— Provide outline and/or one three instructions as you personally "walk them through"

Want others to notice their patient perseverance	— Compliment then for their steady follow-through
Avoid risks and changes	— Give them personal assurances
Dislike conflict	— Act non-aggressively
Accommodate others	— Allow them to provide service and support for others
Look for calmness and peace	— Provide a relaxing, friendly atmosphere
Enjoy teamwork	— Provide them with a coop-erative group/ team
Want sincere feedback that they're appreciated	— Acknowledge their easygoing manner and helpful efforts,

THE CAUTIOUS THINKER:

Have you noticed my efficiency

Goals and fears

Cautious Thinkers concern themselves more with content than with congratulations. They prefer involvement with the performance of products and services under specific, and preferably controlled, conditions so the process and the results can be correct. Since their primary concern is accuracy, human emotions may take a back seat with this type. After all, emotions are subjective and tend to distort objectivity. Cautious Thinkers biggest fears of uncontrolled emotions and irrational acts relate to their goals. More precisely, Cautious Thinkers fear that these illogical acts may prevent goal achievement. Similarly, they fear emotionality and irrationality in others. This type strives to avoid embarrassment, so they attempt to control both themselves and their emotions.

Strengths and weaknesses

Cautious Thinker strengths include accuracy, dependability, independence, clarification and testing skills, follow-through, and organization. They often focus on expectations (e.g., policies, practices, and procedures) and outcomes. They want to know how things work so they can evaluate how correctly they function. We picture a fox as an appropriate symbol for Cautious Thinkers--cagey, resourceful, and careful. Because they need to be right, they prefer checking processes themselves. This tendency toward perfectionism, taken to an extreme, can result in "paralysis by overanalysis". These overly cautious traits may result in worry that the process isn't progressing right, which further promotes their tendency to behave in a more critical, detached way.

Complex and serious

They prefer tasks to people, clearly defined priorities, and a known pace which is agreeable to them, especially where task time lines and deadlines are involved. Other types typically live life through a single predominant time orientation--past, present, or future. But Cautious Thinkers are apt to be concerned about all three, as one aspect of their complex mental makeup. They tend to see the serious, more complicated sides of situations as well as the lighter--or even bizarre side-- which accounts for their natural mental wit.

As the most cerebrally-oriented of the four types, Cautious Thinkers concentrate on making decisions in both logical and cautious ways to ensure that they take best available action. (This cerebral quality refers to the way they process information and experiences, and does not relate to I.Q.) "It's not whether you win or lose. . .it's how you play the game"--the more technically perfect, the better.

Think deeply

Visualize Woody Allen, the quiet, unassuming director, actor, and clarinet player who covets his privacy. In most of his movies, either he or his characters agonize over what to do next, what and how their feelings operate, and how to ultimately do the right thing. He typically puts his emotions under a microscope where he analyzes and reanalyzes them. Cautious Thinkers also can become overwhelmed by indecision when pressure builds.

Due to compliance to their own personal standards, they demand a lot from themselves and others and may succumb to overly critical tendencies. But Cautious Thinkers often keep their criticisms to themselves, hesitating to tell people what they think is deficient. They typically share information, both positive and negative, only on a "need to know" basis when they are assured that there will be no negative consequences for themselves.

When Cautious Thinkers quietly hold their ground, they do so as a direct result of their proven knowledge of facts and details or their evaluation that others will tend to react less assertively. So they can be assertive when they perceive they're in control of a relationship or their environment. Having determined the specific risks, margins of error, and other variables that significantly influence the desired results, they will take action.

Cautious Thinkers entertain uniquely

Cautious Thinker entertainers want to move beyond the audience, since they are motivated to deliver a one-of-a-kind, captivating, near-perfect performance. They want spectators to think, "What a unique performance" or "Nothing else is quite like it!" When they take their varied stages, Cautious Thinker entertainers have meticulously prepared themselves to provide a memorable experience with each intense performance--a key reason why they seem more emotionally drained from their own efforts.

Cautious Thinker countries

Under adverse political and geographic conditions, two Cautious Thinker countries have historically figured out creative, intuitive ways to survive. Both Sweden and Switzerland have harsh winter climates, but they've mastered the art of survival. Switzerland, especially, boasts a substantial corner on the market of world finance. For a small country, it controls a disproportionate amount of the world's money. And Sweden, long known as a land that appreciates beauty, continues to have a worldwide impact in exporting its aesthetic talents, products, and services resulting from cultivated efforts.

Whether watching a professional tennis match or beauty contest, we frequently see a representative from sparsely populated Sweden in the running for top honors. And, whether shopping for distinctive items--such as Scandinavian sweaters, needlework, furniture, crafts or other unique objects--or tasty and eye-catching bakery goods, the artistic flair of the Swedish heritage has universal appeal.

Which of the following Cautious Thinker characteristics listed below match individuals you know with cultural roots similar to those discussed above?

- careful--methodical and cautious; don't jump into things initially

- precise--need to be accurate, so they check and recheck in their effort to find the right or best available answer

- proper-- more formal, discreet, and inclined to allow others to be in their own space, expecting the same for themselves

- private--keep thoughts to themselves; do not willingly disclose their own or others' thoughts and feelings

- reserved--somewhat formal and cool; take time to get to know them--they have few close relationships

- logical--process-oriented seekers of reason

- inventive--like to see things in new or unique ways; often have a perspective that includes or addresses both themselves and others

- contemplative--introverted and reflective, they ponder both the "why" and "how" elements in situations

Action Plan . . .

CAUTIOUS THINKER CHARACTERISTICS	SO YOU . . .
Concerned with aggressive approaches	— Approach them in a Indirect, non-threatening way
Think logically	— Show your reasoning
Seek data	— Give it to them In Writing
Need to know the process	— Provide explanations and rationale
Utilize caution	— Allow them to think, inquire and check before they make decisions
Prefer to do things themselves	— When delegating, let them check on others' progress and performance

Want others to notice their accuracy	— Compliment them on their thoroughness
Avoid conflict	— Tactfully ask for clarification and assistance you may need
Need to be right	— Allow them time to find the best or "correct" answer
Like to contemplate	— Tell them 'why" and "how"

Four types, just acting themselves

With the natural differences among the four behavioral types in mind, pretend that you want to give four people 15-20 minutes to make three simple decisions:

1. Where the next meeting will take place
2. When it will happen
3. The theme of the meeting

Quite by accident, your group consists of one Steady Relater, one Cautious Thinker, one Dominant Director, and one Interacting Socializer who all believe in practicing The Golden Rule. Do you think they'll get the job done? Perhaps, or perhaps not, depending on how each responds to one another in handling the simple task. Let's see why this may not work out. As they walk into the room, the Dominant Director typically speaks first. "Here's my plan. . ."

The Interacting Socializer says, "Hey! Who died and left you boss?"

The Cautious Thinker says, "You know there seems to be more here than meets the eye. We might want to consider some other relevant issues and break into sub-committees to explore them."

The Steady Relater smiles and says, "We may not get this done if we don't work as a team like we have before."

If you think that we're stacking the deck, consider putting all four of one behavioral type into the room to make those decisions. They'd get the job done, wouldn't they? Not if they follow the Golden Rule verbatim!

What do you call it when you send four Dominant Directors into the same room? War!

Or four Cautious Thinkers? A laundry list full of questions!

And four Steady Relaters? Nothing! They sit around smiling at each other: "You go first." "No, why don't you go first. By the way, how's the family?"

When four Interacting Socializers walk out, try asking them if they've gotten the job done. "Get what done?" They've had a party and instead come out with 10 new jokes and stories.

We admit that we may be exaggerating to make a point, but in some cases, not by much. Dominant Directors tend to have the assertiveness and leadership initiative to get tasks started. They may then delegate to others for follow-through, enabling the Dominant Directors to start still other new projects that interest them more.

Cautious Thinkers typically are motivated by their planning and organizational tendencies. If we want a task done precisely, find a Cautious Thinker. Of the four types, they're the most motivated to be correct--the quality control experts.

Steady Relaters have persistence, people-to-people strengths-- patience, follow-through, and responsiveness. When we have a problem, we may choose to go to a sympathetic-appearing Steady Relater because he or she listens, empathizes, and reacts to our feelings.

Interacting Socializers are natural entertainers who thrive on involvement with people. They also love to start things, but often do not finish them. In fact, they may pick up three balls, throw them in the air, and yell, "Catch!" Emotional, enthusiastic, optimistic, and friendly, Interacting Socializers usually pep up an otherwise dull environment.

A behavioral knight-time story

Here is a story to reinforce the differences between the four basic behavioral types:

Four of King Arthur's knights, each representing a different behavioral type, were convicted of a crime and sentenced to death by decapitation. On execution day, they mounted the stairs together to position their heads in a custom-made, four person guillotine. (For you skeptical types who may be wondering why King Arthur uses a French product, maybe it's a gift from King Louis.) The Lord High Executioner swings his royal ax, the rope snaps, and the blade comes down--stopping inches from their necks. King Arthur interprets this as a sign of innocence, so he pardons all four men. They all rejoice--some noisily, some silently--with everyone reverting to his own type of instinctive response.

Almost immediately, the Dominant Director knight turns to the others and yells, "You see! I told you I 'm innocent!"

The Interacting Socializer knight screams, "Let's eat, drink, be merry. . .and party, party, party!"

The Steady Relater knight walks up to the executioner and says, "I want you to know that I don't hold this against you. You were just doing your job and I know you're a good person at heart. Would you like to join me for dinner sometime?"

The Cautious Thinker knight pauses, looks up at the mechanism, scratches his head, and says, "Hmmm, I think I see the problem."

Pick a type. . .any type

After our general introduction to the basic four, core behavioral types, you may already know which one is most like you. Did you also recognize other people you know? Besides deciding which type is most like you, you may have thought of people who sounded quite similar to one or more of the personality types in this chapter--those you harmonize with and those who tend to "rub you the wrong way". Now that you know which type you are, you can better determine other people's types. Integrating what you know about yourself with what you can observe and learn about others reveals valuable information to help you relate more effectively with them. The next chapter explains how to determine other personality types by focusing on specific verbal, vocal, and visual signals they provide. So get ready to become a people reader in Chapter 3.

Remember . . .

TASK ORIENTED

Cautious Thinker

Dominant Director

PEOPLE ORIENTED

Steady Relaters

Interacting Socializers

FASTER PACED

Dominant Directors

Interacting Socializers

SLOWER PACED

Steady Relaters

Cautious Thinkers

WHO SEEKS WHAT?

Dominant Directors

Cautious Thinkers

Interacting Socializers

Steady Relaters

Power & Control

Accuracy & Precision

Popularity & Prestige

Sincerity and Appreciation

KIND OF DECISION MAKER

Dominant Director   Decisive

Cautious Thinker   Deliberate

Steady Relater   Conferring

Interacting Socializer   Spontaneous

Chapter 3
How Will You Know One When You Meet One?

Now that you're familiar with your core behavioral type, how can you recognize other types when you meet them? Since relationships depend on your appropriate interactions with each behavioral type, the immediate question is, "How can I identify someone's behavioral type and how can I do it quickly?"

Two important dimensions for recognizing another person's behavioral type are Directness and Openness. We all exhibit a range of these characteristics in our expressed, observable behaviors. But we need to focus on how people act in order to determine their core type.

"Excuse me, Mr. Smith, but would you mind giving me some information about how Indirect or Direct and how Open or Guarded you are so I can figure out your behavioral type?" definitely won't do. Neither will guesswork, but that approach is seldom necessary because people give so many clues, if you just know what to look for. To identify someone's type, observe what he does by tuning in to both his verbal, vocal, and visual behaviors.

Verbal, vocal, and visual clues

The verbal channel of communication includes the words people use to express themselves—the content. The other two areas convey the intent of the message—how people want to say it. The vocal channel includes all the subtle aspects of voice intonation—volume, speed, resonance, pitch, inflection, and rhythm. The visual channel includes all the aspects of body language—the range of movements and positions—from the subtle raising of an eyebrow to the precise movements of the trained actor.

We have assembled a range of verbal, vocal, and visual characteristics into a list of observable behaviors for each type. But beware! These descriptions refer to actions you can see, not value judgments you may be tempted to make about them. If you see a woman hopping up and down, is it because she is throwing a temper tantrum, has stepped on a nail, has a foot that has fallen asleep, or is very excited? All you can say is she is hopping up and down. Finding out why requires more observable verbal, vocal, and visual clues.

Is the person more Direct?

Directness, the first of two dimensions in our expressed behavior, is the amount of involvement a person uses to meet his needs by seeking to influence people and situations. Directness means the tendency to move forward or act outwardly by expressing thoughts, feelings, or expectations. Direct people come on strong, take the social initiative, and create a powerful first impression. They tend to be assertive, fast-paced people who make swift decisions and take risks. They can easily become impatient with others who cannot keep up with their pace. As active people who talk a lot, they appear confident and sometimes dominant. Direct people tend to express opinions readily and make emphatic statements. Such individuals try to shape their environment and relationships—"Tell McCullough that I want to talk to him ASAP." Indirect people typically act in a more measured way—"I'll get back to you about McCullough, Jack."

Direct people are faster paced, more assertive, and more competitive. At worst, these tendencies can transform into hastiness, combativeness, or lower awareness of others' needs. More outspoken, talkative, and dominant, Direct people are extroverts who focus their attention on interests in their environment. In other words—action! They tend to work and play faster. When at a social gathering, they're the ones who introduce themselves as a natural way of seeking to influence others in their surroundings.

They prefer to make rapid decisions, becoming impatient when things don't move fast enough or don't go their way. Checking for errors is something other people can do. It's too time-consuming and self-involving for Direct people. Instead of checking, they busily rush into new areas where the more Indirect may fear to tread. In fact, they rush into so many new areas that their time seems to evaporate into thin air. That's one reason why they have difficulty consistently being prompt—because something comes up at the office or somewhere else. Meanwhile, their more punctual, Indirect friends learn to busy themselves with time killers, such as projects or magazines, while waiting for their more easily sidetracked companions.

Direct people may enjoy risks and want results now, or yesterday. Risks are a way of life with them. Not only are they less worried about rocking the boat, they'll often tip it over and splash around in the hot water they find themselves in. They crave excitement, so they do as much as possible to get it.

This type feels that if they throw enough against the wall, something has to stick. Who cares if the output isn't perfect! Quantity beats quality (within limits known only to them) most days of the week. So they're likely to tolerate a higher error rate than their Indirect counterparts to gain a higher number of trial opportunities, even if their success ratio is lower. They generally figure that the number of successes is more important than the percentage of successes.

Anyone involved in telemarketing or outside sales realizes that the road to success is littered with setbacks. Direct people excel in these arenas because they're able to take no's; they simply go out and find more prospects. Aware the yes's are out there somewhere, they're determined to unearth them. "The odds are definitely in my favor now. I'm due for a big hit!" Indirect people tend to take those no's as personal rejections, responding by examining other alternatives which don't force them to go out again. "Maybe if I send out a direct mail letter first, then follow up by phone, I'll increase my chances of getting a *yes*."

Direct people point, finger jab, or otherwise more observably express themselves in methods ranging from open arms to forearms—literally, a hug or a shove. They are verbally intense. "This is the way it is, so get used to it." They emphasize their points of view with confident-sounding vocal intonations and assertive body language.

They speak with conviction. "This idiot got an advanced degree from a diploma mill!" Fast-talking, Direct people like to tell, not ask, about situations. If you want to know the answer, just ask them. They can even become brutally blunt— "That's supposed to be a custom suit? It looks more like it's off the rack of a discount store."

Impatient and quick-paced, they jump into things, so they get into more "iffy" situations than their indirect counterparts. Just as the songs of the sirens lured sailors to their doom, the *windows of opportunity* beckon to Direct people. Entrance sometimes nets them huge results and sometimes slaps them with dramatic disasters. Wherever inclination takes them, their natural tendency is to do their own thing.

When the windows of opportunity crack open, the Direct types can't wait to tell somebody. So they seek willing listeners—usually of the Indirect variety—and they say, "I've found a gray area."

What sort of feedback do you suppose the Indirect types probably provide? "It sounds interesting, but it also raises a lot of questions. Have you asked anyone else for their opinion? Your boss, for instance?"

"Ask my boss? Forget it! He might say no! Then what would I do? My hands would be tied."

This more Direct person's motto in these cases is, "It's easier to beg forgiveness than seek permission." When in doubt, do it anyway. You can always apologize later.

Or Indirect?

On the opposite side of the Directness spectrum, Indirect people are more quiet and reserved. They are seen as more easygoing, or at least more self-contained. Indirect people ask questions and listen more than they talk. They typically reserve their opinions. When asked to take a stand, they may make tentative statements. They often appear more objective, quiet, and indecisive. When taken to an extreme, these positive traits can be viewed as negative ones—wishy-washy, tight-lipped, unassertive behaviors. Indirect people are also less confronting, less demanding, less assertive, and less socially competitive than their Direct counterparts. They're team players who allow others to take the social initiative. For instance, when they want to go to the movies or a restaurant, they might think to themselves, "Gee, I'd really like to see that new romantic comedy movie." Then they wait for someone to invite them to go instead of outwardly expressing interest to others.

They tend to be more security-conscious—moving slowly, meditating on their decisions, and avoiding bigger risks. As a result, they often avoid taking bold chances or spontaneous actions. After all, what's the best way to keep from failing? One way is to do nothing until you're satisfied it would be an improvement. In other words, do only sure things. Those sure things result in a higher success ratio, so they are more natural for Indirect people. Number of successes divided by number of tries equals success. In a given month, they may try 10 things. Nine may be successfully completed, one not—for a success ratio of 90%.

When Indirect people flop, they tend to take the setback personally. They are likely to internalize or privately think about it, often wondering if there's something wrong with them. "How could I have been so stupid?" Just give them a hint that something is going wrong, and reserved folks may engage in negative self-talk for days.

Indirect people tend to move at a slower or more measured pace. For them, sooner or later is good enough. They speak and respond more slowly since they are more cautious or stability-focused when considering change. If the behavior becomes too measured, detractors (usually Direct people) can view this as dragging their feet, or even lacking interest.

Predictability is more important to such Indirect people, so they tend to consider the pros and cons, attend to details, and fact-find. Caught in a gray area with no clear-cut guidelines, they usually ask for clarification or permission before they take action. They seek to meet their needs by accommodating the requirements of their environment. Generally they operate according to established formats and rules, so when you make an appointment with an Indirect person, you can expect him to show up on time, or possibly wait for you!

Indirect people tend to communicate by asking instead of stating. Their questions clarify, support, or seek more information—"By that, do you mean . . . ?" They prefer qualified statements—"According to my sources, the candidate received an advanced degree from a non-accredited university." They speak more tentatively and take a roundabout or step-by-step approach—"It seems to me that this is so." If they don't like something, they respond subtly—"Well, I think your other suit looks better." They reserve the right to express their opinions or keep them to themselves. But, they can also act like impregnable rocks when they don't want to crack.

Some are more, some less

It is important to realize that people vary in their location on this scale of Direct to Indirect behaviors. Think of someone you know who irritates you. Now that you know about Direct and Indirect characteristics, have you figured out which trait best describes him or her? One important consideration is to determine the person's preferred pace. Pace refers to natural rate of speed—whether he does things quickly or slowly. Bearing in mind pace and other trait descriptors for Direct and Indirect people, let's determine whether that person is more Direct or Indirect. Nobody fits exactly in the middle.

You may be wondering which are better—Direct traits or Indirect ones. We can answer with an unqualified, "It depends." Sometimes it's better to act more Direct and sometimes it's better to act more Indirect. Comparing the two is like evaluating San Diego and New York City. Each is very different, yet we could build a strong argument in either one's favor.

Appropriateness depends on the requirements of a situation. The real question isn't which is better, but how to best use the positive aspects of each trait while recognizing accompanying less developed attributes. Since each of our lives involves a variety of situations requiring differing responses, remember there is no one best personality type. The idea is to maximize people's natural traits while understanding and trying to minimize their accompanying drawbacks.

Survey of Directness versus Indirectness

This is an informal survey designed to provide you with a general description of how you see others in daily situations. Answer as objectively as possible. This is a non-judgmental assessment—there are no right or wrong answers. Choose one person you know (socially, personally, or at work) and answer these nine questions in terms of how you see that person most of the time, in most situations. This will help you determine if this person is more Direct or Indirect. For each number, choose the one statement that best applies to the person you are evaluating.

Is the Person More Direct or Indirect?

1. (I) A less frequent contributor to group conversations OR

   (D) A more frequent contributor to group conversations

2. (I) Tends to keep personal thoughts or feelings private, sharing only when asked and necessary, OR

   (D) Tends to express personal thoughts or feelings about things, whether asked to or not

3. (D) Frequently uses gestures, facial expressions, and voice intonation to emphasize points, OR

   (I) Less likely to use gestures, facial expressions, and voice intonation to emphasize points

4. (D) More likely to make statements: "That's the way it is!" or, "I feel . . ." OR

   (I) More likely to ask questions or speak less assertively: "How does this fit?" or, "As I understand it ..."

5. (I) More likely to wait for others to introduce him (or her) at social gatherings, OR

   (D) More likely to introduce self at social gatherings

6. (I) Tends to remain involved with known situations, conditions, and relationships, OR

   (D) Tends to seek new experiences, situations, and opportunities

7. (D) Likely to express own views more readily, OR

(I) Likely to reserve the expression of own views

8. (I) Tends to react more slowly and deliberately, OR

   (D) Tends to react more quickly and spontaneously

9. (I) Likely to respond to risk and change in a more cautious or predictable manner, OR

   (D) Likely to respond to risk and change in a more dynamic or unpredictable manner

Total number circled: D's_____ I's_____

(Directness)   (Indirectness)

Open or Guarded

Besides Direct to Indirect behaviors, we've also found that people tend to be either Open or Guarded—the other major dimension that describes our daily actions. Basically, Directness and Indirectness describe people's observable behavior—how others see and hear us behaving. The second behavioral scale explains the motivating goal behind these daily actions. Why we do the things we do in the way we do them. When combined, these two scales explain both the tendencies to reveal our thoughts and feelings plus the degree to which we tend to support other people's expressions of their thoughts and feelings.

Is the person more Open?

If he talks with his body, uses more vocal inflection, makes continual eye contact, and speaks in terms of feelings, then he's projecting more Open than Guarded behaviors. Other Open cues that show greater responsiveness include animated facial expressions, much hand and body movement, a flexible time perspective, and immediate non-verbal feedback. Open people also like to tell stories and anecdotes and make personal contact.

Open people are more open to responding to digressions than Guarded personalities are. They need to make conversation more enjoyable, so they look favorably upon straying from the subject to discuss personal experiences. As long as it's in the ballpark, they figure it's probably relevant. "That reminds me of the time Uncle Jed got stuck on the Garden State Freeway for five hours . . . " And exaggeration of details just adds interest by fully depicting their experiences.

Open types are also more negotiable about time. Their time perspective is organized around the needs of people first and tasks second, so they're more flexible about how others use their time than the Guarded types. "I'm sorry I'm late for work today, but my son was crying this morning because Jason broke his science project. So I had to write a note to the teacher and cheer him up before I dropped him off at school."

Of course, like any behavior that's overused, these same Open characteristics can also drive people up the wall if they get out of hand. For example, self-disclosure can be seen as neediness, digression as inattention, animation as melodrama, acquiescence as weakness, and friendliness as patronization. As with Direct to Indirect tendencies, too much of anything can become a liability.

Or Guarded?

If Open types seem more like open books, then Guarded ones tend to be more *poker faced*. Guarded individuals prefer to play their real cards closer to the vest— increasing the probability of getting the upper hand and decreasing the probability of appearing foolish. They usually like to keep their distance, both physically and mentally. They don't touch you and you don't touch them. People often say this about a Guarded person they know: "Once you get to know him, he's a really great guy." But you must become acquainted by breaking through that exterior shell that he erects. Consequently, Guarded people tend to stand further away from you, even when shaking hands. They have a strong sense of personal space and territory, so make sure you don't take anything from their desks. At home they might set traps with a rug or a sofa cushion to see if someone used them when they weren't supposed to. You know—the tiny fold in the rug or the perfectly aligned pillow on the couch. "You sat on that couch today, didn't you? I asked you not to go in my room when I'm not there. I have proof that someone walked on that rug and sat on that couch."

Guarded people show little facial expression, use controlled or limited hand and body movement, and adhere to a more time-disciplined agenda. They push for facts and details, focus on the issues and tasks at hand, and keep their personal feelings private. They don't touch, and they tend to respond coolly if anyone touches them. Unlike their Open counterparts, they give little non-verbal feedback.

By contrast, Guarded types place higher priority on getting things done. They prefer working with things or through people—rather than with or for them. "I can't talk now, Frank. I have a two o'clock deadline to meet," or "I'll let you know when I have time to do that," are characteristic comments of this pattern.

Guarded people like structure, since they expect results within that structured environment. When negatively motivated, these types of individuals can be viewed as coercive, restrictive, or overbearing. They prefer to stick with the agenda, at least their own. As more naturally independent workers, they need to control the conditions around their tasks—either in terms of input and output (Directness) or the process itself (Indirectness). These more self-contained people make use of either key talent or key procedures to meet their goals. Thus, they view the planning and supervision processes as ways of reaching goals. The Direct individuals need to control people while the Indirect types need to control their environment.

Because time equals money to Guarded people, they're more disciplined about how other people use their time. In part, this explains their tendency not to show, discuss, or willingly listen to thoughts and feelings like Open people. Guarded people are more matter-of-fact, with more fixed expectations of people and situations. Just as facts place second for Open people, feelings take a back seat for Guarded people. You might say that Open people experience life by tuning in to the concerns or feeling states (of themselves and others) and then reacting to them. Guarded people focus on the points or ideas in question.

Guarded people like to know where a conversation is going. Idle, non-directed chitchat is not for them. If Open types stray from the subject, Guarded people find a way to bring them back on track. They usually need clarity before they move on to the next topic. If you get off the subject, they're likely to ask, "Can you sum that up for me?" or, "What is the key point you're trying to make?"

Because of their different priorities, Guarded types can perceive more Open ones as time wasting or wishy-washy. And Open people may view these Guarded people as cold, unsympathetic, or self-involved. As a result, misunderstandings can quickly grow out of proportion when we don't discern and respond to these types of differences. You may still wonder which is better—Open or Guarded behavior. And again, the answer is, "It depends." As with Directness and Indirectness, circumstances determine the appropriateness of any type of behavior. Our awareness of potential pitfalls for each personality pattern can save multitudes of problems for ourselves and others as well as for our workplace, social groups, and organizations.

Whereas Open people may feel any attention is better than no attention at all, Guarded people tend to be more selective about whom they associate with. They feel more comfortable retaining firm control over their emotions.

Ranges of behavior

Whether a person is more Open or Guarded, remember there are degrees of these characteristics that vary from individual to individual. When the chips are down, Open people tend to spare others' feelings at the expense of completing a task. Guarded people want to get things done, even though feelings may get hurt as part of the emotional cost of accomplishment. This does not necessarily mean that Open people do not believe in responsibly doing their work; it just means that people are a higher concern. Similarly, it does not mean Guarded people do not value other people. They simply think the best way to deal with people is by a more controlled style of behavior.

Survey of Open versus Guarded Behaviors

Follow the same guidelines for this set of nine questions as you did for the Direct and Indirect ones earlier in this chapter. Focus on the same person that you did previously.

Is the Person More Open or Guarded?

1. (S) More open to getting to know people better and establishing new relationships, OR

   (C) Exerts more control over who he/she gets involved with, including how well you get to know them

2. (C) Focuses conversations on tasks, issues, business, or subject at hand, OR

   (S) Allows conversations to take the direction of interest of the parties involved, even though this may stray from the business or subject at hand

3. (C) Tends to make decisions based on objectives, facts, or evidence, OR

(S) Tends to make decisions based on feelings, experiences, or relationships

4. (C) More likely to expect and respond to conflicts, OR

   (S) Less likely to expect conflict and more motivated to personally deal with conflicts when they arise

5. (S) More likely to accept others' points of view (ideas, feelings, and concerns), OR

   (C) Less likely to accept other people's points of view (ideas, feelings, and concerns)

6. (C) Tends to focus mostly on the idea, concept, or outcome, OR

   (S) Tends to focus primarily on the interest level, persons involved, and process

7. (S) More open about own time involvement with others, OR

   (C) Less open about own time involvement with others

8. (C) Likely to stick with own agendas and concerns while tuning in to the power motives of others, OR

   (S) Likely to tune in to others' agendas and concerns while minimizing any conflict or disagreement

9. (C) Prefers to work independently or dictate the conditions as it involves others, OR

   (S) Prefers to work with and through others, providing support when possible

Total number circled: C's_____   S's_____
                      (Guarded)   (Open)

To identify a person's behavioral style

Simply use the process of elimination. If the person is more Direct than Indirect, then you can eliminate the Steady Relater and Cautious Thinker types (the two Indirect styles). If the person is also more Open than Guarded, then eliminate the Dominant Director (the more Guarded type). Now you arrive at the remaining style, in this case, an Interacting Socializer.

Which type is this?

You have an appointment with a client whose secretary sets the time for exactly 10:10 a.m., not 10:00 or 10:30. After acknowledging you in the reception area with a fixed, polite smile, she gives several detailed instructions to her secretary. Gathering behavioral clues, you notice that she dresses impeccably. She again smiles politely at you and asks you to follow her into the office. She tells you where to sit, checks her watch, and actually says, "You have exactly 15 minutes. Go."

During your presentation, the client remains as expressionless as a statue in a museum. No emotion shows. She asks for highly specific facts, assesses your responses, and then extends the discussion in areas of interest to her. She invites you to stay longer and literally closes the sale herself after getting specific answers to her time, schedule, and cost questions.

There are many clues to help you determine the behavioral style of this client. First, look at her Direct versus Indirect behaviors. You can be fairly sure of placing her as Direct: She directs the conversation, confronts the issues head-on, controls both you and the situation (when to begin, where to sit, what to discuss), and closes the sale herself. That's Directness!

Next, look at her Open or Guarded tendencies. By nature of her time discipline, fact and task orientation, formality, and expressionless face, she is fairly easily to classify as Guarded.

When you put together the two aspects that determine behavioral style, you have a combined rating of high Directness/low Openness. These two classifications tell you that the client is a Dominant Director.

One more time

You conduct a seminar that begins at 8:30 a.m., following an 8:00 coffee and doughnut session. When you arrive at 7:45, the first participant is already seated in the room, pad and pencils neatly lying in front of her. She says nothing until you approach. Then she politely shakes hands. She is totally noncommittal. You ask a few questions and receive polite, short answers.

Around 8:15, with several other people in the room, a person stops hesitantly at the door and softly asks, "Excuse me. Is this the training seminar for salespeople?" When he hears, "yes," he breathes a sigh, walks in, takes a cup of coffee, and mentions how interesting he hopes the seminar will be, saying it really could be helpful in business and at home. He asks a few questions, listening intently to other's remarks. He expresses some concern for role-playing in front of a group.

At this moment, another participant strides in, loudly asking, "Hey, is this the sales seminar?" Upon hearing, "yes," this person dramatizes relief and asks where the coffee is, explaining that he can't function without caffeine. He has overheard the role-playing comments and leaps in on the conversation to say how he likes doing those things. He follows this with a tale of how he embarrassed himself in the last role-play session he attended.

Which style is the first person? The second? The last?

The first person's apparent disinterest in conversation and restrained gestures identify her as Indirect. This narrows the possible choices to either a Steady Relater or Cautious Thinker. She is also clearly in control of her emotions and the setting—Guarded, as opposed to Open. Another name for an Indirect/Guarded person is a Cautious Thinker.

The second participant speaks with a soft voice, requests clarification, and hesitates before starting the seminar. All these clues add up to an Indirect behavior pattern (Cautious Thinker or Steady Relater). He volunteers information about personal feelings and gives rapid feedback with his sigh and comments. These are Open characteristics. This person shows a Steady Relater style.

Participant number three demonstrates Directness through his speed of response, fast movements, and high quantity of conversation (Dominant Director or Interacting Socializer). He also shows Open behaviors by telling stories and responding quickly. These are traits of the Interacting Socializer.

How Will You Know a Dominant Director When You See One?

At the office

When entering Dominant Directors' offices, look around. The overall tone suggests authority and control. Their desks may be covered with projects and papers, stacked in neat piles. Both their in- and out-baskets typically bulge with busywork. They tend to surround themselves with trophies, awards, and other evidence of personal achievement. Virtually everything about the place suggests hustle, bustle, formality, and power. This type is the one that often favors a large chair behind a massive authority structure known as a *power desk*. Besides nonverbally announcing, "I'm important," the desk separates them from visitors, literally keeping them at a distance.

Notice the walls

The walls may include diplomas, commendations, and other evidence of success. One wall may have a large planning sheet or calendar on it . . . the better to juggle with, my dear. If Dominant Directors have family photos, they may hang behind them or someplace where they don't readily see them. To this type, their offices are places of business and the fewer distractions they have, the better.

Hustle, bustle, and busywork

Dominant Directors like constant activity, so you'll seldom catch them idle. Between existing tasks, they pick up new ones. They perk up when competing and appear to thrive with a pressure cooker schedule. They often squeeze you onto their calendars and let you know that their time is limited, either by telling you outright or by showing you. Looking at a watch or clock, they frequently shift their gaze elsewhere, or make and take phone calls while you sit in their office.

They walk fast in pursuit of a tangible goal, so Dominant Directors may not notice people around them or may just hurriedly grunt something to acknowledge them. They often act both brisk and brusque without realizing it. When under stress, impatience emerges and they may push others aside to reach their goal—completing a report, getting served first, or running out the door to make an appointment. When pressure intensifies, Dominant Directors often rise to the occasion. Under time constraints, they may concede to impatience and rely on educated guesses, even their own hunches.

Power symbols

Dominant Directors tend to dress comfortably and typically pay less attention to their appearance than the other types. They may program themselves primarily for work results, so wardrobe tends to play a secondary role in most fields of work. They may be candidates for a timesaving personal shopper or tailor who can choose or measure outfits for them in the privacy of their own offices. Dominant Directors gravitate toward authority symbols, so they may wear navy blue or charcoal gray *power* suits.

Dominant Directors may like to let people know they've *made it* without having to tell anyone about it, so they often prefer possessions that emit success and authority messages— like a black or steel gray Mercedes or BMW. Someone once suggested they'd buy a tank, if they could.

Observable Characteristics of Dominant Directors

Verbal	Vocal	Visual
States more than asks	More vocal variety	Firm handshake
Talks more than Listens	More forceful tone	Steady eye contact
Primarily verbal, not written, communication	Communicates readily	Gestures to emphasize points
Makes strong Statements	High volume, fast speech	Displays impatience
Blunt and to the Point	Challenging voice intonation	Fast moving body language

How Will You Know a Dominant Director by Phone?

When speaking on the phone to a Dominant Director, treat her the same way as in a person-to-person contact. Think of the ABC's: Keep it abridged, brief, and concise. Then we prepare our delivery with the bottom line in mind: "The trend in your industry is toward computer-generated graphics. The research we've conducted with other type-setters in your area indicates increased profits of 20 to 30% over two years. I'd like to meet with you for 10 minutes to show you the numbers and see if this concept interests you."

They waste no time

It's not unusual for a Dominant Director to call someone and, without saying hello, launch right into the conversation. "You've got to be kidding; the shipment from Hong Kong will kill us . . . by the way, this is Jack." When other people can't keep up with their speed, they may view them as incompetent.

On the telephone, determine whether the person sends power signals. Dominant Directors want to pick the time and place to meet. They often speak in a sort of shorthand—concisely and pointedly—and sound cool, confident, and demanding. When Dominant Director Dennis phones, he actually says: "Janice? Dennis. Tony there?" Talking to him is like speaking to a human telegram. He reduces the concept of *brief and to the point* to another dimension. As commanding speakers who tend not to listen to others, they naturally want to direct the conversation toward their goals. Under stress, they can become defensive and aggressive, attacking others personally to show who's in control. They dislike using *touchy-feely*, emotional terms and prefer sensible *thinking* terminology. "I think we'll implement this plan tomorrow," or, "I think this discussion is over."

Their letters are brief and to the point

A letter from a Dominant Director tends to be brief, forceful, and to the point. They may mention highlights of conversations or materials, but they don't belabor them. They may give specifics for your follow-through or raise questions they want answers to now. "The Mulvany account needs to be reworked. I hear he's got a new partner and a different address. Track him down and get the data we need so we can let him know that we've studied his account and we know our stuff."

Even notes and cards take on abbreviated forms and may show little or no indication of feelings. "Todd, hope you're doing well. I'm working hard . . . " We know more than one Dominant Director who signs personal birthday and Christmas cards with no closing, not even *Sincerely*, but with just their names. Steady Relaters and Interacting Socializers gravitate more toward *Warmly*, *Fondly*, or *Cordially*. But Dominant Directors, perhaps in their efforts to get as many things accomplished as possible, tend to opt for brevity.

Pick a Dominant Director co-worker

Think of a co-worker who is a strong Dominant Director in the workplace. What characteristics does he or she exhibit that reveal those Dominant Director traits? How do you get along with this person? Why?

How Will You Know an Interacting Socializer When You See One?

At the office

When you enter the working area of an Interacting Socializer, look around his office. What does it look like? Even if you've never been to this type's office before, you may recognize it from across the room. Interacting Socializers may strew paperwork across their desks, sometimes trailing it along the floor, too. They react to visual stimuli, so they like to have everything where they can see it. Consequently, their desks often look cluttered and disorganized. If anyone comments, "How do you find anything?" they like to say that they're *organized in their disorganization.*

And the walls?

Interacting Socializer walls may sport prestigious awards. They may be broad, liberal arts degrees, motivational or upbeat slogans, generalized personal comments, or stimulating posters. You may see notes posted and taped all over the place with little apparent forethought, rhyme, or reason. Overall decor reflects an open, airy, lively atmosphere that often reveals the personality of its occupant. Likewise, the furniture arrangement tends to indicate warmth, openness, and contact. An Interacting Socializer seldom sits behind a desk when he talks. He often opts for comfortable, accessible seating, enabling him to meet his goal of getting to know people better. He prefers to sit next to us at a table or on a couch so he can see and hear us better and get a feel for how we respond to him. He talks a lot and shows emotion with both his body language and speech.

Feelings take priority

Interacting Socializers have a natural preference for talking and listening in *feeling* terms. Unconsciously, they may become uncomfortable when talking to a person who, instead, uses *thinking* words. (The opposite also is true). Statements like, "I feel that we should have been consulted about moving our office," or, "I feel good about what we've accomplished today," tend to put this people-oriented type more at ease.

They like glitz and pizzazz!

The way Interacting Socializers dress often relates to their need for recognition. Since they like others to notice them, they may dress in the latest style. *Look at me* Socializers like bright colors and unusual clothes that prompt others to compliment them. Many Interacting Socializers even prefer negative comments to none at all. "Are you dressed for Halloween today, Rhonda?" At least she's getting the attention she craves.

In an informal poll taken by Dr. Tony at his many seminars, red ranks number one with Interacting Socializers as their color choice for a sports car or convertible. They like glamour, flash, and excitement . . . and their purchases often express their preferences. Musical choices even include energizing songs like *Celebration*.

Observable Characteristics of Interacting Socializers

Verbal	**Vocal**	**Visual**
Tells stories, anecdotes	Lots of inflection	Animated facial expressions

Shares personal feelings	More pitch variation	Much hand/body movement
Informal speech	More variety in vocal quality	Contact oriented
Expresses opinions readily	Dramatic actions	Spontaneous
Flexible time	High volume perspective	
Digresses from conversation	Fast speech	

How Will You Know an Interacting Socializer by Phone?

"What's up?" or "What's happening?" are usual Interacting Socializer opening lines. They are sometimes so animated that their gestures can be transmitted via the phone lines. How? By their varied, emotional vocal inflections/intonations and their colorful choice of words that may tend toward exaggeration. "Really? That's fantastic!" or, "You have to be kidding me!" The telephone can be a favorite toy that enables them to both prolong conversations and recharge themselves, especially when no one else is physically around. "I just called because I'm bored." You may also detect background noise when you speak to individuals of this type. They sometimes put on the TV or radio just for the sound, visual stimulation, and activity.

On the phone, Interacting Socializers speak rapidly and emotionally. "I feel that if we go through with this plan, the community will resent us as anti-environmentalists," or, "I feel that I've contributed enough to this organization over the years to allow me to talk about this." Other styles may more naturally use *thinking* words, instead.

Say it with feeling

Typically, you'll notice a wide range of vocal inflection and intonation and a tendency to want to know your reaction. "Do you feel that way, too?" They liven up conversations with personal anecdotes and may keep you on the phone longer than you had anticipated. If you need to extricate yourself from an extended monologue, try something like, "Well, Don, it's been great talking with you. I'm really looking forward to our appointment on Monday!" If you say it with feeling, the Interacting Socializer may already eagerly anticipate your meeting.

By Letter?

Letters, too, can reveal the Interacting Socializer behind the correspondence. Often, this type overuses exclamation points, underlining, and bold highlighting. You can almost hear her emphasizing those picturesque adjectives and adverbs. Just as the Interacting Socializer tends to speak in a stimulating, energetic way, so does she write. She may also throw in an image-provoking personal anecdote or reference to some mutually satisfying experience. "I'll never forget our adventure on the freeway en route to Los Angeles—in rush hour, of course!" When she's finished a letter or note, she may add a postscript (P.S.), a P.P.S., or even a P.P.P.S.

Caution: Again, these tendencies may not as readily reveal themselves if the Interacting Socializer has learned to tone down her natural flair while conducting business. And there's always a possibility that the secretary *cleans up* her copy before typing it out, especially if she is a more exacting, less animated behavioral type.

How Will You Know a Steady Relater When You See One?

Office memorabilia

When you enter a Steady Relater's office, be alert for conservatively framed personal slogans, group photos, serene landscapes and posters, and other personal items. Since they seek close relationships, also look around for telltale family pictures and mementos, usually turned so they can view them from their desk chair. They often favor nostalgic memories of stabilizing experiences and relationships in our increasingly high tech world. These remembrances of a pleasant, uncomplicated past allow them to transform their offices into an environment of friendly, warm ambience. They prefer to arrange seating in a side-by-side, more congenial, cooperative manner. No big power desks for them! If they do have one, though, they'll typically come out from behind it to *reach out* by opting for a more personal touch.

Service certificates

Their educational background often includes more specialized areas of attention and interest within their professions. You may also see certificates recognizing volunteer hours for various hands-on activities in their community. While other behavioral types may contribute in other ways—such as gifts of money—Steady Relaters typically enjoy giving their time for causes they feel strongly about. Besides the possibility of meeting more potential friends, this also helps satisfy their need to see for themselves: (1) what's really going on, (2) where they fit into the group effort, and (3) how they can get meaningful, concrete results.

Steady Relaters are natural listeners

You can recognize Steady Relaters by their natural listening patterns and slower, lower-key delivery. Their questions often focus on concrete topics and experiences. "What did you say the terms for payment were again?" They walk casually; acknowledging others and sometimes getting sidetracked by chance encounters.

Nothing too loud for them

Steady Relaters dislike calling attention to themselves, so they tend to wear subdued colors and conservatively cut clothing, favoring conventional styles that don't stand out too much. Their cars also reveal these preferences. They often like beige or light blue vans, factory recommended tires, and in the best of all worlds—no horn. To Steady Relaters, using a horn is like yelling at somebody. Steady Relaters often tell us they like mellow, soothing, easy listening music.

Observable Characteristics of Steady Relaters

Verbal	Vocal	Visual
Ask more than State	Steady, even-tempered delivery	Intermittent eye contact
Listen more than talk	Less forceful tone of expression	Gentle handshake
Reserve opinions	Lower, quieter volume	Exhibit patience
Less verbal communication	Slower rate of speech	Slower moving body language

How Will You Know a Steady Relater by Phone?

"How are you?" or "I'm glad to hear from you again," are typical Steady Relater greetings. Like those telephone company TV commercials, their warmth can seem to transcend the limitations of the phone lines. Although they prefer more personal interactions with people, they will also settle for indirect contact—especially if the person is pleasant and non-threatening. They project this people orientation by phone and like to build a personal, first name relationship with callers. Even if they don't know you, they may say, "You don't have to be formal. Just call me Alice." They may project a desire to know you personally or provide you with good service.

They communicate with steady, even vocal intonations to convey friendliness, comfort, and a sense of relaxation. Steady Relaters tend to be naturals at listening to others' ideas and feelings, whether on the phone or in person. They tend to be interested in the blow-by-blow, point-by-point description of what you did yesterday or the sequential pattern of how to complete a certain task. You're probably talking to a Steady Relater if you notice slower than average speech patterns, more moments of listening than of speaking, and references to actual, real-life experiences regarding either products or mutual acquaintances.

"I'll look it up for you"

Steady Relaters tend to express themselves in a rather tentative manner in both their face-to-face and telephone conversations. "I'll need to consult Mrs. Adams before I can make that decision," or, "I'm not sure we can do that, but I'll get back to you as soon as I find out." As in other aspects of their lives, they often defer to the more human, proven way things have always been done. They typically feel more comfortable making decisions based on conferring with others rather than by themselves. "What do you think?" and "How do you feel?" and "What do you recommend?" are all common questions this type may ask.

When They Think About Someone, They May Drop a Line

In their written correspondence, Steady Relaters may send letters just to keep in touch or to let you know they're thinking of you. Of the four personality types, this one is likely to send thank you notes for almost anything—inviting them to a party, driving them to the dry cleaners, or saving coupons for them. They may even send a thank you note to acknowledge your thank you note. Again, they are likely to organize their letters, writing as they do their other *to do* task lists—probably in sequential *in-out* order. Since they tend to write in a slower, more methodically paced manner, their work tends to follow a systematic outline pattern.

Visualize a Steady Relater friend

Picture a friend of yours who best typifies the Steady Relater. What does he or she do that fits the type? How do you tend to interact with him or her?

How Will You Know a Cautious Thinker When You See One?

At the office

Cautious Thinkers often carry their organizational tendencies into their work environments. Environmental clues include neat, highly organized desks with cleared tops so they can work unimpeded by clutter—clean, shipshape, and professional with everything in the appropriate place. Charts, graphs, exhibits, models, credentials, and job-related pictures are often placed neatly on their office walls or shelves. Cautious Thinkers favor a functional decor that will enable them to work more efficiently. They tend to keep most objects within reach, readily available when needed. Where appropriate, you may notice state-of-the-art technology to further enhance efficiency.

Cautious Thinkers ask pertinent questions

People of few words, Cautious Thinkers tend to ask pertinent questions instead of making statements. They typically speak more carefully and with less expression than the other types. Reluctant to reveal personal feelings, they often use *thinking* words (like the Dominant Director), as opposed to *feeling* words. "From what I've read, I think Product X may be better for our situation than Product Y because of its superior filtration system," or, "I think that Jones is overreacting in this matter."

Formality is more comfortable

Cautious Thinkers are non-contact people who prefer the formality of distance. This preference is reflected in the functional, but uninviting arrangement of their desks and chairs, usually with the desks physically separating you and them. They generally are not fond of huggers and touchers, and prefer a cool handshake or a brief phone call. When Cautious Thinkers walk, they usually move slowly and methodically toward a known destination.

Noticeably understated

Cautious Thinkers tend to wear more conservative clothes, but with unique, often perfectly matched accessories. While the Interacting Socializer may draw attention to himself with glitz and glitter, Cautious Thinkers usually prefer a more understated, faultlessly groomed look with nary a hair out of place. But their taste may differ from the people around them.

They like expressions of individuality and creativity, but within guidelines. For some reason, male Cautious Thinkers with beards seem to prefer short, well-manicured ones. If they smoke, they often prefer pipes—perhaps, someone noted, this is because taking a puff from a pipe gives them more time to think before they answer. Since they may prefer exploring life's complexities, they may enjoy the intricacies of a specific kind of music or individual musical piece, whether jazz, classical, rock, etc. You may spot them driving well-built, practical cars that perform well, often in more conservative, understated, but less common colors.

Observable Characteristics of Cautious Thinkers

Verbal	**Vocal**	**Visual**
Fact and task-oriented	Little inflection	Few facial expressions
Limited sharing of feelings	Few pitch variations	Non-contact oriented
More formal	Less variety in and proper	Few gestures vocal quality
Focused conversation	Steady, mono-tone delivery	Slower moving
Less verbal, more written	Lower volume, slower speech communication	

How Will You Know a Cautious Thinker by Phone?

"Good afternoon, Mr. Lomis. This is Jonathan Williams. You asked me to call back Monday morning." Formal greetings are one tip-off that you may be dealing with a Cautious Thinker. Time-conscious individuals of this type often get to a task just when they say they will. Monday morning it is! In this example, the Cautious Thinker also calls himself Jonathan, not Jon. We've noticed that many people in this category call themselves by their given names, not by nicknames. It's Elizabeth, Rebecca, Donald, and Peter, not Beth, Becka, Don, or Pete. Of course, there are exceptions. Actually, Jon may prove to be an effective and logical alternative for some Cautious Thinkers, but this type seems less likely to tolerate what they perceive as cute nicknames for themselves, such as Johnny, Ricky, Cindy, or Becky.

"May I speak with Mr. Holmes or Spock from Star Trek?"

They prefer brief, to-the-point telephone calls. Although they may not tell you, call them Mister or Ms. or Doctor or whatever their titles happen to be. Cautious Thinkers sometimes view jumping into a first-name basis as invasion of privacy, so they deal with others on a more formal basis. If you think you're talking to Sherlock Holmes or Spock, chances are you've contacted a Cautious Thinker. They typically retain their ground in stressful situations when they can maintain their position with concrete facts or reverse-control questions. They do this quietly and independently, by first avoiding others. Then they take on the problem in an orderly way that is aligned with their own plan.

"Need to know" basis

They're inclined to talk in rather structured, careful speech patterns, almost weighing their words as they say them. They tend to ask pertinent questions and talk in a quiet, observant, cautious way. Additionally, they may not volunteer much about their personal selves beyond the equivalent of name, rank, and serial number. "Yes, I'm married with two children. We live in New York." They prefer to keep the relationship formal, yet pleasant and businesslike. Less can be more to a Cautious Thinker—less conversation, self-disclosure, and verbal communication equals more comfort zone. So we must learn to hear between the lines: Longer than average silences, especially when we ask them more private questions, may signal annoyance or reluctance. When this occurs, ask, "Am I getting too personal?" or "If I'm asking uncomfortable questions, how could you let me know so I don't make a problem for either of us?" They may relax more if they think they have an out.

Careful and correct

Like Steady Relaters, Cautious Thinkers tend to express themselves in a rather tentative manner. "I'll check on that and let you know tomorrow." Or they may want to provide you with information so you can form your own conclusions. "I have a copy of the Governor's report in my files. If I send it to you, perhaps you can find what you're looking for." Both these approaches satisfy Cautious Thinkers' need for caution and correctness. They simply may not want to get misquoted or, possibly, involved in the first place.

How Will You Know a Cautious Thinker by Letter?

Cautious Thinkers typically send letters to clarify or explain positions. Consequently, these letters may become rather long and filled with data. "I was struck by the similarities between the Noonan and Kilgary lawsuits." But they may also be somewhat reserved or vague. "I'm researching a company's file now that I literally can't talk about." Or the letter may be on the short side with enclosures, citings, or references to specific information. Whether they prefer the long or short form, they usually concentrate on processing data. They like to cover their bases so they are neither misinterpreted, incomplete, nor incorrect.

Like Dominant Directors, in the interest of time, they may sign personal cards with just their names or with individual mottos, like "In the spirit of growth, Jonathan Williams." Even if you know them well, this type may include their surnames so there's no mistaking who sent this card.

If the shoe fits

The dimensions that determine type—Direct/Indirect and Guarded/Open—have their own innate strengths and weaknesses. In fact, the strengths are closely allied to the weaknesses—the strengths taken to an extreme. The Direct-Guarded type can become overbearing when he pushes persistence too hard. Similarly, the Direct-Open type may turn manipulative; the Indirect-Open type, wishy-washy; or the Indirect-Guarded type, unreachable. These and other positive or negative characteristics shade the actions of all four types. Individuals representing all four may have the same assignment, but use different approaches. If a monthly report is due, one type may keep a day-by-day journal (Indirect-Guarded), another may delegate the work (Direct-Guarded), another may prefer completing it with a co-worker (Indirect-Open), and yet another may prefer to pull an *all- nighter* to complete it at the last minute (Direct-Open).

By now, you know how to recognize the four core types by observing environmental clues and external behaviors. The four combinations we've just discussed—Direct/Guarded, or Dominant Director; Direct/Open, or Interacting Socializer; Indirect/Open, or Steady Relater; and Indirect/Guarded, or Cautious Thinker—all behave differently from each other in various situations. Whether at home, work, a social activity, or in a romantic encounter, they all naturally act true to their own type. It's their attempts to fill their type's needs and expectations. By acting themselves, they show their true core behavioral colors.

In the next chapter, *Adaptability*, you'll read about getting along with all the behavioral types in their natural, and less natural, life environments. You'll learn how to have more productive relationships with people of all types.

DISTINIGUISHING CHARACTERISTICS
OF THE FOUR STYLES

STEADY *RELATER*	CAUTIOUS *THINKER*	DOMINANT *DIRECTOR*	INTERACTING *SOCIALIZER*
1) BEHAVIOR PATTERN			
Indirect/Open	Indirect/Guarded	Direct/Guarded	Direct/Open
2) PACE			
Slower/Relaxed	Slower/Systematic	Faster/Decisive	Faster/Spontaneous
3) PRIORITY			
The Relationship/ Communication	The Task/ Process	The Task/ Results	The Relationship/ Interaction
4) FEARS			
Sudden changes, Instability	Personal criticism of their work efforts	Being taken advantage of	Loss of social recognition
5) GAINS SECURITY THROUGH			
Friendship, Cooperation	Preparation, Thoroughness	Control, Leadership	Playfulness, Other's approval
6) MEASURES PERSONAL WORTH BY			
Compatibility with others, Depth of contribution	Precision, Accuracy, Quality or results	Impact of results, Track record	Acknowledgment, Applause, Compliments
7) INTERNAL MOTIVATOR			
The "Participation"	The "Process"	The "Win"	The "Show"
8) APPEARANCE			
Casual, Conforming	Formal, Conservative	Businesslike, Functional	Fashionable, Stylish

DAILY EXAMPLES OF THE FOUR STYLES

STEADY RELATER	CAUTIOUS THINKER	DOMINANT DIRECTOR	INTERACTING SOCIALIZER
1) SEEKS			
Acceptance	Accuracy	Control	Recognition
2) STRENGTHS			
Listening	Planning	Administration	Persuading
Teamwork	Systematizing	Leadership	Enthusiastic
Follow-through	Orchestration	Pioneering	Entertaining
3) WEAKNESSES (GROWTH AREAS)			
Oversensitive	Perfectionist	Impatient	Inattentive to detail
Slow to	Critical	Insensitive	Short
begin action		to others	attention span
Lacks global	Unresponsive	Poor listener	Low
perspective			follow-through
4) IRRITATIONS			
Insensitivity	Disorganization	Inefficiency	Routines
Impatience	Impropriety	Indecision	Complexity
5) UNDER STRESS			
Submissive	Withdrawn	Dictatorial	Sarcastic
Indecisive	Headstrong	Critical	Superficial
6) DECISION MAKING ATTERN			
Conferring	Deliberate	Decisive	Spontaneous
7) OCCUPATIONS			
Family doctor	Engineer	Executive	Sales
Social services	Researcher	Military leader	Public relations
Teacher	Artist	Newspaper editor	Actor

Chapter 4
Creating Personal Power Through Behavioral Adaptability

What is it?

Behavioral adaptability is the key to success with the different types. With adaptability, we can treat the other person the way he wants to be treated. We define it as the willingness and ability to engage in a range of behaviors not necessarily characteristic of your style in response to effectively dealing with the requirements of a situation or relationship. Behavioral adaptability is something applied more to yourself (to your patterns, attitudes, and habits) than to others. It involves making strategic adjustments to your methods of communicating and behaving, based on the particular needs of the relationship at a particular time. Adaptable people try to meet the expectations of others by practicing tact. They make the choice to go beyond their own comfort zone so others feel more comfortable—especially with the derived results.

What adaptability isn't

Adaptability does not mean imitation of the other person's behavioral style. It does mean adjusting your Openness and Directness in line with the other person's preference. At the same time, it means maintaining your own identity and good sense. You modify your spots.

So does that mean that Cautious Thinkers prefer the company of Cautious Thinkers and that the other types prefer people who share their type? Yes and no. Two clichés apply. *Birds of a feather flock together*, and *Opposites attract*. Dominant Directors may personally admire other Dominant Directors like themselves for their accomplishments and success rates, but prefer to be more guarded with them at work in order to maintain their own power and authority.

Cautious Thinkers may appreciate Interacting Socializers for their joy of life, but steer clear of them at work because of their imprecision. Interacting Socializers may enjoy Cautious Thinkers for their command of matters of interest to them, but may stay aloof at work because of the Cautious Thinkers' desired perfectionism. Steady Relaters and Dominant Directors may also admire each other's qualities or feel alienated by them. So what's a person to do?

Remember that the willingness to try behaviors not necessarily characteristic of your type is called *behavioral adaptability*. It is not the same as your behavioral type. No members of any type corner the market on adaptability. No style is *naturally* more adaptable than another. In other words, Steady Relaters as a group are no more adaptable than Interacting Socializers, Dominant Directors, or Cautious Thinkers (and vice versa).

Your adaptability level affects the way other people perceive you. Raise your adaptability and you'll discover trust and credibility go up; lower it, and they go down. Behavioral adaptability means adjusting your behavior to allow others to be more at ease, encouraged, and successful in your relationship.

Which style is most adaptable?

No one style is naturally more adaptable than another. For a given situation, the strategic adjustments each behavioral style makes will vary. The decision to employ specific techniques of behavioral adaptability is made on a case-by-case basis. You can choose to be adaptable with one person and not with another. You can also choose to be quite adaptable with one person today and less with that same person tomorrow. Behavioral adaptability concerns the way you manage your own communication and behaviors. It also involves how you manage the requirements that exist for a task or situation—whether other people are involved or not.

For example, when an Interacting Socializer works with a Cautious Thinker on a common task, one of the ways she can practice behavioral adaptability is by talking less, listening more, and focusing on the critical facts. Behavioral adaptability means adjusting your own behavior to make other people feel more at ease with you and the situation. You practice adaptability every time you slow down for a Cautious Thinker or Steady Relater—or when you move a bit faster for an Interacting Socializer or a Dominant Director. Adaptability occurs when the Dominant Director or the Cautious Thinker takes the time to listen to a human interest or family story told by an Interacting Socializer or a Steady Relater.

The Adaptability Recipe

Adaptability is a phenomenon that has many characteristics. In fact, formal research studies in which we have been involved have identified at least 10 such attributes of people who are highly adaptable and 10 characteristics of those who have lower adaptability—a total of 20 traits in all. Of course, no person is likely to be either totally adaptable or non-adaptable. Instead, each of us possesses:

- different general, overall levels of adaptability ranging from higher (more characteristic) to lower (less characteristic)

- personal differences in various situations regarding our level of the two basic ingredients of adaptability— flexibility and versatility

- specific key strengths and possible growth areas in the 20 behaviors which make up your overall level of development in adaptability potential

The 10 behaviors which define the person with high adaptability potential are different from behavioral type, so anybody can choose to enter the higher range characteristics of a more enlightened, functionally mature human being. Unfortunately, the 10 at the lower end represent the darker side more characteristic of lower order animals and species. But you (and every other individual) have the personal power to increase your level of adaptability if you are willing to learn the abilities to get there.

The high and low adapters

The research conducted on flexibility has shown you view yourself as both more flexible and versatile than you actually are. In part, this is because you aspire toward who and what you want to be. As a result, your view of yourself includes both how you intend to act and how you actually do act. However, the reality of how you act is based only on the second element.

Another factor that explains this gap in our idealized versus actual level of adaptability is that it's not easy. If you're like most people, you may not be aware of all 10 behaviors that allow you to achieve your potential, let alone have already developed them as personal strengths. Similarly, you may not have thought about the 10 others that undermine your potential strengths. Here are all 20, broken down into 10 flexibility strengths and weaknesses and 10 versatility plus and minus points.

Higher flexibility is characterized by these personal attitudes:

- confidence—the attitude of belief in one's self, trusting your own judgment and resourcefulness

- tolerance—open-minded state of acceptance; willingness to defer judgment on the basis of limited time or information

- empathy—sensitivity to another's point of view; caring approach towards others (without being overwhelmed or manipulated by people)

- positiveness—maintaining a state of positive expectations about people and situations, including a positive state of energy in your thoughts and emotional patterns

- respect for others—desire to understand, accept, and consider mutual and separate interests, choices, and commitments

Lower flexibility is characterized by these personal attitudes:

- rigidity

- competition with others

- discontent

- being unapproachable

- difficulty in dealing with ambiguity

Just think of the more successful individuals you have admired, both personally and from afar, and you'll probably notice your list is full of people with high flexibility strengths. Those with lower flexibility characteristics seldom seem to make the cut.

Now, for the other half of this adaptability formula— versatility. Our research indicates people have a more clear-cut understanding, and generally a higher developed level, of flexibility than versatility. Versatility, instead, involves a set of personal aptitudes which are distinctly different from merely being willing to adapt. Many people are willing to modify their behaviors, but simply lack the required set of abilities. Versatility is a complex set of mental and emotional abilities that we acquire over time through a variety of sources. These include formal education, daily life experiences, and observations of others who demonstrate these same behaviors.

The good news is that versatility can be learned. People aren't born either high or low in versatility. But more versatile people tend to approach every situation in each day of their lives as new opportunities for learning and growing. And, of course, others make a personal decision to opt for the lower road—getting the consequences that go along with the easier way of doing things in life.

Higher versatility is characterized by these personal aptitudes:

- resilience—learning how to cope in spite of setbacks, barriers, or limited resources

- vision—foresight, creativity, and imagination

- attentiveness—being mindful and aware of stimuli in the environment; reality-focused

- competence—capability of managing required tasks and being knowledgeable about required subjects and people; including uses and updates of appropriate abilities

- self-correction—able to initiate and evaluate by oneself, seeking feedback as appropriate, characterized by a problem-solving mind set/approach to matters

Lower versatility is characterized by these personal aptitudes:

- subjectiveness

- bluntness

- resistance

- single-mindedness

- unreasonable risk-taking

Flexibility

The flexibility dimension of adaptability is the half that involves your personal attitudes toward yourself, others, and the situations you face. It indicates your degree of willingness to change your perspective and/or position, when appropriate. Examples follow of a lower and higher level of adaptability in a person, and the way each one is likely to respond.

Here's a brief summary of some of these key differences between such people:

Higher flexibility attitudes indicate . . .

- a higher level of security and sense of personal worth or well-being

- an open-minded, searching attitude in dealing with people and situations

- positive expectations about your own goals and desired results, and those of others

Lower flexibility attitudes indicate . . .

- a tendency to be reactive to people, conditions, or events—often responding out of fear or anxiety

- predetermined views, conclusions, or patterns of behavior which are non-negotiable

- a tendency to be negative about what may occur, especially if points of view or opinions change

As you review the following statements, you can see the differences in higher versus lower flexibility.

Lower personal flexibility

"What do you expect of me? That's just the way I am. It's me . . . my type of person or style I'm stuck with . . . so I can't do anything about it."

Higher personal flexibility

"Well, one thing I've learned is that each of us can be our own worst enemy in our own unique way. That's the real benefit I've gained from this *type* kind of behavioral style idea. Now, I realize my more natural strengths, preferences and short suits. As a result, I've made conscious efforts to monitor these to make sure they stay in the positive range while also learning how I can become better by modifying myself, at times."

Lower personal flexibility

"Look, each of us has our own cross to bear in terms of other people. I can't be expected to get along with everyone. There are such things as personality conflicts and that's all there is to it. So I try to seek those people I get along with and stay away from all those other types that pose problems for me—and themselves, too."

Higher personal flexibility

"Obviously, since no two people are identical and there are few Prince Charming/Cinderella matches in the real world, each of us has to work at our relationships if we want them to be mutually satisfying. This means I have to be willing to accept every person as worthwhile, regardless of their style or values. The key is being willing to understand as well as accept them as people I want to get along with. When I do, I've found that things usually work out quite well; and when I don't, then it usually doesn't. The choice and the consequences belong to me."

Lower personal flexibility

"Look, I'm just your average, hard-working kind of person. I mean, I'm good at handling some types of situations, and not so successful with others. But I've learned to accept this fact. After all, nobody's perfect. So I just don't deal with those situations that pose problems for me. Instead, I either avoid them or try to get someone else to handle them. After all, why should I get all bent out of shape about these?"

Higher personal flexibility

"I consider myself a lot more effective as a person—both at work and in my personal life—because I've learned how to adjust my own preferred style of doing things when it gets in the way of the kinds of results I want to achieve. This has been a real breakthrough for me and has given me a much greater sense of confidence in my ability to deal with situations that arise."

Versatility

By comparison with flexible individuals, highly versatile people demonstrate a set of distinctive abilities in realistically and productively managing a variety of situations. This includes the stresses that accompany this higher activity level. In addition, their actions are clearly goal oriented, serving a meaningful purpose in their own personal aspirations, their relationships with others, and the desirable outcomes of situations. They also exhibit appropriate problem-solving actions that match the requirements that exist in dealing with a broad range of different situations.

Lower versatility is characterized by a tendency to be responsive only to one's personal preferences or expectations, discounting the reality of other factors that require consideration. As a result, these people tend to be more one-dimensional in their behavior. If they are Open and Direct, for instance, they have difficulty demonstrating other behaviors, even when different actions are more appropriate in a specific situation. Additionally, while they tend to be very adept at finding problems and passing them off to other people, they lack the same skillfulness when it comes to contributing to the solution of such problems.

Higher versatility individuals

Employee: "One of the things I really like about my job is that every day is different. I'm always learning something new and have the opportunity to respond to many types of situations where I can use my talents as well as develop other ones. In fact, our company gives us the chance to take a variety of training programs—both in-house and through continuing education programs—and they reimburse us for part of the cost. I'm always on the lookout for ones that fill in the gaps for my job and areas where I'd like to get better."

Homemaker: "I used to work before I had children, but now I really enjoy being at home. There are a wide variety of tasks and challenges I face in the job my husband calls chief executive officer of our home. We have three children, and as you might guess, each of them is quite different. My husband is, too. That significantly impacts the way I organize schedules, and respond to the many little stresses each one faces, from their own point of view. I also keep an eye on the bigger picture involving where we were, are, and want to go individually and as a family. That's sure a full-time job, requiring a lot of different skills to understand and manage the range of situations which arise."

Lower versatility individuals

Teenager: "I hate school. It's always the same old thing, day after day and year after year. About the only really good thing about it is I get a chance to meet a lot of people and get invited to a lot of great parties and things. In that way it's a lot better than just sitting around. But I don't really see how a lot of the stuff they try to teach us is really going to apply to what I do. After all, I have a part-time job at a local store and I don't really need hardly anything they teach me to get the things done that they expect of me. So, what's the point?"

Manager: "You know, one of the problems with people nowadays is that they expect a lot more than people did in the good old days. Back then, people just came to work and did what they were told. Even customers were satisfied with what they got as long as it worked and the price was fair. But now the whole world seems to have turned upside down. As a manager, I've got to also deal with a lot of other things that I didn't before. One of the most difficult is knowing how to deal with all of these different expectations which have dramatically changed the nature of the business we're in and how I have to do my job—handling all these people and their concerns. I just do the best I can at this point and try not to make too many waves, but it's confusing. I can't say I'm real clear as to what's expected of me nowadays, let alone how to do these things."

These comparisons indicate that you do not have to be a prisoner of your own behavioral tendencies and patterns. Instead, by increasing your personal flexibility and versatility, you can gain personal success and effectiveness by managing yourself, your relationships, and the situations you encounter. You are in charge of whether you choose to be a person with higher or lower flexibility and versatility.

Everyone can become more adaptable

So the good news is you can, in fact, become more adaptable. The accompanying bad news is that it doesn't happen overnight, by wishing for it, or without occasional regressions back to the old behaviors you felt more comfortable with. Since adaptability involves learning techniques of mind over matter, you can speed up the process and increase your probability for success by focusing once again on the matter of who you are. Coming full circle, this means dealing with who you are. It also means personally committing to work toward overcoming these easier, more natural behaviors you will occasionally slip back into. After all, you've done them thousands of times more than these newer, competing behaviors.

Just as you consult a map when you swerve off course, you can remind yourself to stay on the road to adaptability when you fall back into your old habits. The *Road Map to Personal Adaptability* will help you increase your own flexibility and versatility. You can also use it to coach and assist your friends, family, co-workers, and others through the same learning process. Again, this process begins with who you are. From there, you can work on either those appropriate attitude changes or aptitude changes to develop the potentials related to your own unique behavioral tendencies.

Here's how to use your own road map. First identify your strongest behavioral tendency ("D", "I", "S", or "C"). Select just one goal—either flexibility or versatility—not both at once. Then look across the appropriate row and under the corresponding column to find what you can do to further develop yourself.

Since we don't behave in a vacuum, these general self-adaptations can obviously be further refined for greater success when used more selectively with some types of individuals, and less so with others. Here, then, is a brief *to do* list for ready reference use in deciding what specific types of adaptations are more appropriate when you are interacting with each of the four types of different individuals.

These four basic development action strategies for increasing flexibility and versatility are a good starting point for increasing your own effectiveness. But based on the natural human condition, they tend to be ongoing challenges. Therefore, a second approach that complements this lifelong road map focuses on one of the many adaptability strengths noted above.

To see how this might work, picture some well-known characters who are generally agreed to be lower in either flexibility or versatility. The classic TV character Archie Bunker is a great example of low flexibility. As we review the prior list of higher flexibility strengths, notice how Archie could improve his relationships and his management of situations if he chose to work at developing four of the five strengths mentioned: tolerance, respect for others, empathy, and being more positive.

Action Plan . . .

Steady Relaters

Cultivate a casual, easy going, personable, one-on-one relationship. Treat them with warmth and sensitivity.

Cautious Thinkers

Use an orderly, logical, accurate approach which zeroes in on the process and procedures. Give them well thought-out, accurate documentation.

Me

Dominant Directors

Get right to the point and decisively without getting bogged down in minute details. Operate with conviction, know what you're doing, and don't try to bluff.

Interacting Socializers

Show your energy and liveliness while focusing on the give-and-take interaction. Make your encounter fun, upbeat and enjoyable!

Creating Personal Power Through Increased Adaptability

A wise person once commented, "A little knowledge can be a dangerous thing." In the field of formal education, this quote is sometimes called the sophomoric syndrome. That is, as people begin to learn about a new topic, they tend to jump to oversimplified and incomplete conclusions. When that happens, they are often less successful than is possible. But with continuing effort, thought, and increased study, they eventually graduate to a higher level of excellence. In terms of adaptability, this means it is essential for us to understand the following principles:

1. Adaptability is not a goal in and of itself, but a means to the end of increased personal effectiveness and success.

2. A key to effectiveness is to realize what level and type of adaptability component(s) are the critical factors in achieving a targeted goal.

Examples:

"The key to getting this sale is to be a lot more flexible than I am naturally with this type of strong-willed person."

"If I don't lower my already high tendency to be overly flexible and accommodating, I'm likely to continue giving away the store. Conditions have changed and I can't afford to do that any longer because it conflicts with the results I'm looking for."

3. Being adaptable also means assessing the other available resources that can allow you to get your desired outcomes by acting smarter.

Example:

While you have developed the competencies required to successfully complete a known task, you work with three other people who also possess these same talents. But they don't have the same pressing, competing priorities facing them as you. So in this case, adaptability also includes having the vision and self-corrective aptitudes to seek one or more available resources to help you appropriately manage your adaptability. Isn't that better than trying to be superhuman and doing it all yourself?

Adaptability, then, is important because it directly relates to your degree of achieved success in a wide variety of life's opportunities. These range from relationships with other people, to coping with changing conditions around you, to managing different types of situations.

Extreme behavior can raise others' tensions

At times people may perceive extreme adaptability as acting wishy-washy, sashaying back and forth across the fence line, or acting two-faced. Additionally, a person who maintains high adaptability in all situations may not be able to avoid personal stress and ultimate inefficiency. This was suggested previously by the superperson myth of doing it all yourself. There is also the danger of developing tension from the stress of behaving in a foreign manner with others. This is usually temporary and may in fact be worth it if you gain rapport with the other person.

The other extreme of the continuum is no behavioral adaptability. This causes people to view someone as rigid and uncompromising. He insists on behaving at his own pace and priority.

Adaptability is important to successful relationships of all kinds. People often adopt at least a partially different role in their professional lives than they do in their social and personal lives. This is to successfully manage the professional requirements of their jobs.

Interestingly, many people tend to be more adaptable at work with people they know less and less adaptable at home with people they know better. Why? People generally want to create a good impression at work, but at home may relax and act themselves to the point of unintentionally stepping on other family members' toes. Not an attractive family portrait, but often an accurate one.

We can gain a better understanding of how adaptability impacts the effective management of situations by looking at its application to a variety of professions and their related role or job requirements. This process is essentially the same one that is used by major selection, recruiting, and career development consulting firms around the world.

A sales job which involves a single, simple product line is most likely to require high flexibility, but may not require much versatility. Another sales job involving multiple products that are complex and changing usually requires both high flexibility and high versatility. Contrast this with the position of nuclear researcher that requires very high versatility, but much lower flexibility. This lower flexibility actually protects this person and others from being open to trying possibilities that may literally blow up in their faces. Finally, picture the job requirements of a single working parent of two teenagers. Here again, versatility is the key ingredient in managing the myriad of competing expectations and demands. Of course, a moderate level of flexibility allows the lid to stay on so peace and order prevail and the children don't end up parenting the adult!

Adaptability works

Effectively adaptable people meet the key expectations of others in specific situations—whether it's in personal or business relationships. Through attention and practice, you can achieve a balance of strategically managing your adaptability by recognizing when a modest compromise is appropriate. You'll also understand when it's necessary to adapt to the other person's behavioral style.

Practice managing relationships in a way that allows everyone to win. Be tactful, reasonable, understanding, non-judgmental, and comfortable to talk to. This results in a moderate position between the two extremes. You're able to better meet the needs of the other person as well as your own. Adapt your pace and priority. Work at relationships so everybody wins at work, with friends, on dates, and with family.

So self-knowledge of how Direct/Indirect and Open/ Guarded you are provides help in better dealing with yourself and others. Just as you discovered your own unique behavioral type and the characteristics that go along with it, you'll learn to identify others' key strengths and weaknesses. Recognizing *sterling traits* and potential pitfalls of diverse people means you can better understand their behaviors and relate more effectively with them.

When you try to accommodate the other person's expectations and tendencies, you automatically decrease tension and increase trust. Adaptability enables you to interact more productively with difficult people, helps you in strained situations, and assists you in establishing rapport and credibility. It can make the difference between a productive or an ineffective interpersonal relationship. And your adaptability level also influences how others judge their relationships with you. Raise your adaptability level—trust and credibility soar; lower your adaptability level—trust and credibility plummet.

Another way of looking at this whole matter is from the perspective of maturity. Mature persons know who they are. They understand their basic behavioral type and freely express their core patterns. However, when problems or opportunities arise, they readily and deliberately make whatever adjustments are necessary in their core patterns to meet the need. Immature persons, on the other hand, lose effectiveness in dealing with the real world when they lock into their own style. By disregarding the needs of others, they end up causing conflict and tension that lead to less satisfaction and fulfillment in their life environments.

There are four key payoffs which make our efforts at becoming more mature and adaptable worth the effort. These benefits define the characteristics of people who are the higher performers in life. By reading, reflecting, and then taking the guided actions suggested in this book, you too can achieve this same level of excellence in your own life. The only questions are whether you wish to become more:

- successful

- effective

- satisfied

- fulfilled

If so, then today is your first opportunity to get started based on what you've already learned in these first four chapters. Now you can read the remaining chapters for even more powerful insights about how you can become all that you can truly be.

Chapter 5

On the Job

Problem solving in the workplace

As you read this chapter, think of specific individuals you know at work who represent each of the four behavioral styles—Dominant Director, Interacting Socializer, Steady Relater, and Cautious Thinker. How can you apply what you learn about them to improve your working relationships with each one? What are some characteristics that work to the advantage of these people in their job performance? Which characteristics work against them?

All jobs essentially involve different types of problem-solving tasks that have to be achieved to ensure satisfactory job performance. And, since such job requirements differ, so too does the degree of natural match or fit with your own preferred behavior pattern. As jobs become more complex, they call for increased adaptability to fulfill these job expectations which may be quite different from your own sources of natural inner motivation. Let's look further at how adaptability is critical in influencing these four behavior patterns. The graphic entitled "Our Problem-Solving Work Styles" provides you with a summary illustration of the four distinctly different types of problem-solving approaches to your daily work efforts.

Dominant Director Behavior in a Work Setting

Preferred jobs

Higher power positions and career areas where they can take charge

- President or CEO; i.e., the formally recognized leader

- Politician

- Policeman/woman

- Military officer

- Executive or manager

- Entrepreneur

- Owner of his or her own company

- General contractor

"I'll solve that problem"

A typical Dominant Director point of view consists of seeing himself as a problem-oriented manager who enjoys a challenge just because it's there. He likes the opportunity to complete tasks in a creative manner—which aligns with his way, of course! He's independent, strong-willed, restless, and goal-oriented. Other people tend to view him as having a high level of confidence, although this may not be the case. However, when he reads something he doesn't understand, he may instinctively react as if it must be a misprint. His self-image is high, and so is his output.

Because of their drive for specific and concrete results, Dominant Directors often put in extra hours at the office. At the extreme, their high results-orientation can manifest in an overextended work pattern. When this happens, they pay a high price for their success—their personal and social lives may fall apart from neglect while their work-related attainments accumulate.

Dominant Directors can juggle faster than the eye can see

When the Dominant Director perceives others' output as less than exemplary, he may react with a message to stimulate others to action: "Don't just stand there. Do something!" Dominant Directors typically show administrative and leadership qualities that reflect their ability to initiate and accomplish tasks, then juggle them.

They have the ability to pick up three balls (tasks) and keep them all in the air at the same time. They're multi-phasic behavior specialists—able to simultaneously do many things well. After adapting to juggling three balls, they pick up another and another. They end up juggling all of them faster than the eye can see where one begins and the other ends. However, the pressure mounts as they try to maximize the quantity of tasks or the quality of results.

Logically, it makes sense to drop one ball to relieve some of the pressure. Not so with the Dominant Director. Admission that they can't do it all tarnishes their macho image. They like impressing other styles with their workloads until they get bored or tired of not-enough-hours-in-the-day balancing acts. Then they drop everything to take up a new direction or focus for their activities until they tire of the same pattern again. Dominant Directors typically refer to this as reordering priorities.

Efficiency is the name of the game

Adult Dominant Directors often like to accumulate items—especially ones they think will save time or money. Efficiency is the name of the game. One Dominant Director told us he's so impatient that he never buys green tomatoes. Another one is exhilarated by the fast-forward feature that lets her eliminate the time taken up by TV commercials as she plays her Tivo. A third enjoys using her hands free cell phone so she doesn't have to waste time while driving; she can't wait to get others to implement her ideas.

Despite their strongman images, Dominant Directors, too, have their own unique limitations. They're selective listeners who tend to tune out small talk. To increase their adaptability, their listening skills and awareness of others' needs require improvement. Instead of telling others what to do, hearing their thoughts and opinions can help them get things done more smoothly—for the good of everyone involved. Otherwise, people may interpret the Dominant Director's behavior as, "When I want your opinion, I'll give it to you."

Consequently, Dominant Directors tend to work more favorably with complementary types who contribute stability, predictability, and support towards their common objectives. Each of these other types can help the Dominant Director put tasks into perspective, recharge his or her batteries, or bolster a temporarily bruised ego. Other people's feedback can also help Dominant Directors stay on track in terms of objectivity, accuracy, and responsiveness to others' needs.

D leaders

The Dominant Director is an outspoken, no-nonsense, take-control type of individual. Give 'Em Hell Harry Truman summed up the Dominant Director's work-style attitude with his now famous statement: "If you can't stand the heat, get out of the kitchen." In fact, many Presidents of the United States have shared this same Dominant behavioral tendency with Harry. They include John F. Kennedy, Franklin D. Roosevelt, and Ronald Reagan. Each of them exhibited a personal need to decisively lead—including their willingness to use force to do it, if required. And each of them preferred the roads to the most direct action for fast results. When under stress, they lashed out and forcefully took charge in differing ways. All can be described as either strong, hard to budge, or both.

Generals George Patton and Napoleon Bonaparte, two Dominant Director military leaders, depict this "Go for the gusto!" "No guts, no glory!" perspective of their type. In battle, Dominant Director mottos translate to Charge! or Follow me! but not necessarily in that order. When taken to the extreme, Dominant Directors may, at times, seem to live by the watchwords, "Ready! Fire! Aim!" because they tend to naturally plunge in without a lot of risk-assessing forethought.

They may not be too busy for that, after all

Sometimes others may interpret the Dominant Director's hustle and impatience as, "Don't interrupt me. I'm busy." Ironically, when this happens, the Dominant Director may sabotage the very control that he desires. If co-workers and employees perceive him as swamped with too much work, they may hesitate to disturb or delay him. So the Dominant Director may know less about what's happening than he would if he had made himself more accessible.

Risk-taking excites Dominant Directors.

Dominant Directors don't feel as bound by conventional practices as the other types. "That's for other people, not me." The higher authority they prefer to answer to is themselves; they sense a need to be their own boss so they can have control over the results they want. Opportunities for change are sought or created just to satisfy their need for results. They gravitate toward high-risk situations because the excitement of challenges fuels their actions.

They may combine pleasure with business

Dominant Director Dan decided to give his employees a special surprise for Christmas—a combined business/pleasure trip to Honolulu.

From bus excursions to daily seminars and discussion groups, Dan arranged everyone's itinerary. He thought his staff would eagerly embrace his plans, but was extremely disappointed to overhear a few of them complaining about his fixed agenda:

"Who does he think he is? Giving us a supposed vacation and bouncing us around in workshops and seminars, not to mention spending every breathing minute with him!"

"Yes, I know what you mean. Just once, I wish he'd ask us what we want instead of doing what he wants."

"Here, here!"

Dan's first impulse was to rush in and tell those ingrates a thing or three, but he held himself back and decided to call his wife Jean to tell her what happened:

"I can understand their point, Dan. It sounds as though they just want to be part of the decision-making process instead of your telling them what to do," Jean observed.

"Hmmm. I guess the way I did it could seem a bit autocratic."

"I'm glad you see it that way, Dan," said Jean.

"Maybe I'll call an informal meeting so they can let me know just what they want," Dan decided.

So he did. The employees thanked him, but also told him they'd like a few days just to be with their families without having to check in with anyone but themselves.

"Is that all?" Dan asked. The group agreed. "This was a lot easier than I thought it would be," Dan observed.

Fortunately, Dan put himself in his employees' shoes and became willing to see their point of view—they wanted to help decide. For Dan, it seemed much easier to make the decisions and then tell everybody else to follow through. But what he wanted and what they wanted didn't necessarily match.

We know an elementary school principal who chose to manage her school in typical Dominant Director fashion—her way. She decided to arbitrarily rescind the privilege for parents to request teachers for their children because reading all those forms *wasted her secretary's time.* The parents had different ideas and became angry they hadn't been consulted. The resulting furor could have been prevented if she had only stopped to ask, "What do you think?" Actually, she didn't even have to do what the parents wanted, so long as she got their input. They resented her *dictatorial approach.*

The principal, following her Dominant Director instincts, focused on the result, not the steps leading to it. To accomplish that end, she tried to shape the environment by overcoming the opposition. Unfortunately for her, she discovered the parents didn't necessarily want their environment shaped, especially without their feedback. Even benevolent dictators collide with their subjects when they try to rule by themselves.

People, products, and profits

Lee Iacocca, a former CEO who had a Dominant Director work style, talks about how he learned to merge his temperament with other styles as he finally arrived at the following management philosophy, as described in his biography, *Iacocca*: "In the end, all business operations can be reduced to three words: people, products, profits. People come first. Unless you have a good team, you can't do much with the other two." Iacocca, a Dominant Director legend, illustrates the fact that collaborative team playing pays off for Dominant people and others!

Hail to the chief!

Since he views himself as a chief, not just one of the tribe, the Dominant Director may resist deeper involvement in work teams. Stress, especially, brings out his natural apprehensiveness about people. When under duress, he may even seize control and make himself the leader—his natural *me first* tendency.

Consequently, the Dominant Director needs a co-worker who draws him into the group. Dominant Directors often take themselves too seriously and can benefit from gentle reminders to take life less seriously and laugh at themselves.

Competition motivates Dominant Directors

Because he's so competitive, he may view himself as participating in perpetual contests with others. Other styles may see themselves as merely giving reports—period. Not so for the Dominant Director. His report jockeys for position against yours. He needs to have control, so one-upmanship can become one of his favorite games. In this extreme Dominant Director game, he fills the role of the all-seeing, all-knowing expert. Everyone else, by contrast, becomes a babbling idiot. Not a particularly appetizing thought for the rest of us.

Dominant Directors can learn how to occasionally walk away

He can also help himself by learning when to walk away from a project and let others assume control. Otherwise, his tendency to hold on can frustrate the other types. People also tend to respond more favorably to the Dominant Director when he verbalizes the reasons for his conclusions and paces himself to project a more relaxed state. He can also soften his propensity for reprimanding others by tempering criticism with healthy doses of genuinely appreciative praise. Otherwise, about the only time you'll hear a Dominant Director say, "Well done!" is when he orders a steak.

Remember, people have feelings

As natural doers, they may need some help channeling their energies. Why? Because they may have trouble distinguishing the realistic from the awe-inspiring. Of all the types, this one is the most likely to try even harder if told, "That's impossible."

When Dominant Directors learn to become aware of other people's feelings, they become more successful in developing satisfying relationships with them. Since this type has a natural inclination toward authoritarianism, he can work on recognizing when it's appropriate to consciously back off, slow down his fast pace, and listen more to other people's opinions, ideas, and concerns. Besides bolstering his people skills, he can also attend to analyzing tasks more thoroughly. He instinctively wants to hurry on to the next challenge, but he can ward off many problems that result from his typical hastiness by learning more details about projects than he would otherwise seek out.

Other behavioral types may not share the Dominant Director's preferences for quick results and blunt straightforwardness. By becoming less rigid in his direct approach with others, he can better learn to manage the differences between people and modify his own.

Remember...

DOMINANT DIRECTOR BUSINESS CHARACTERISTICS

- Prefer time frames

- Seek personal control

- Get to the point

- Strive to feel important and be noteworthy in their jobs

- Demonstrate persistence and single-mindedness to reach a goal

- Express high ego strength

- Prefer to downplay feelings and relationships

- Focus on task actions that lead to achieving tangible outcomes

- Implement changes in the workplace

- Tend to freely delegate duties, enabling them to take on more projects

DOMINANT DIRECTOR:

PREFERRED BUSINESS SITUATIONS

- Like to call the shots and tell others what to do

- Like challenging workloads which fuel their energy levels

- Tend to personally oversee, or at least know about, their employees' or co-workers' business activities

- Like to say what's on their minds without being concerned about hurting anybody's feelings

- Enjoy taking risks and being involved in changes

- Prefer to interpret the rules and answer to themselves alone

- Interested in the answers to what questions, not how ones

- Like to see a logical road toward increasing and ongoing advancement, since bigger is better to them

At Work with the Interacting Socializer

Preferred job positions

Careers that maximize influence with people where they can socialize, mingle, and gain positive feedback

- Public relations

- Entertainment—acting, singing, reporting, public speaking —being on stage or in the public eye

- Professional host or hostesses (talk show, party, restaurant, airline, etc.)

- Recreation director

- Politician

- Personnel interviewer

- Salesperson

People are their business

The Interacting Socializer likes to be treated with warmth, friendliness, and approval. Because he favors interacting with people on more than just a business level, he wants to be your friend before he does business with you. If a client suggests meeting for lunch, a social drink, or dinner and asks things like, "What exciting things are happening with you?" you're probably dealing with an Interacting Socializer.

Like the Dominant Director, the Interacting Socializer shares a quick pace. While the Dominant Director busies himself with tasks, the Interacting Socializer tends to move about the office in a flurry of activity. He even walks in a way that reflects his optimism and quick pace . . . lively and energetically. He observes and "sight-sees" as he goes, avoiding obstacles and potential problems.

Interacting Socializers like to bounce ideas off others

Interacting Socializers think out loud. Desks confine them, so they typically stroll around the office talking to nearly everyone, from the custodian to the boss along the way, calling them by their first names. All the while they seek others' reactions to almost anything and everything, but they visibly warm up to comments about themselves.

Non-Interacting styles may view Interacting Irv's behavior as goofing off. "That Irv spends more time gabbing at the soda machine than he does working. What does he get paid for, anyway?" But appearances may fool us. While Irv weaves his way toward a drink, he bounces ideas off the people along the way. "John, if you got a coupon in the mail for free dessert at Cafe Eduardo's with any dinner for two, would you go? I'm working on new advertising possibilities for them. What would motivate you to try a new restaurant?"

Irv often doesn't merely talk—he actually brainstorms out loud with virtually anyone he encounters. It's important for him to find out how other people feel about his ideas. He likes the feedback and the occasional pats on the back that his conversations provide. He enjoys a casual, relaxed environment where he can allow his impulses free rein. Desk hopping also satisfies his need for companionship. Like other Interacting Socializers, he seeks out people to first share the present, with one eye on future additional experiences with them. Talking with co-workers happily mixes business with pleasure for this type. They like to play and mingle as they learn, earn, and do practically everything else.

Interacting Socializers seek "people power" positions

Since the Interacting Socializer is naturally talkative and people-oriented, these positions of people power meet his needs for inclusion by others, popularity, social recognition, and (probably) freedom from a lot of detail. They utilize his natural strengths. As with the other types, jobs do not equal behavioral type; but many Interacting Socializers tend to gravitate toward people-oriented, high visibility professions to fill their innate needs.

Disneyland seems to hire vast numbers of Interacting Socializers who act as peppy and people-oriented at 10 p.m. as they did at 10 a.m. Tour guides usually still smile and carry on verbal repartees with guests at the end of their shifts. This characteristic cannot be taught; employees either become energized by mingling with people, or they don't. Interacting Socializers do. Disneyland even provides people-free *decompression* areas for their employees during breaks so they can maintain their positive energy levels with guests.

They're smooth-talking dreamers

At heart, the Interacting Socializer is a dreamer who is good at getting others caught up in his ideas. His persuasive powers may simultaneously amaze his admirers and frustrate his detractors. The Interacting Socializer shows smooth-talking tendencies which, at the extreme, can be interpreted as either silver-tongued oration or evasive double-talk. He can appear to be a verbal Pied Piper with a seemingly unending gift of gab or a wheeling and dealing chatterbox.

Chin up!

As a leader, the Interacting Socializer likes spontaneous, expressive actions for noticeable results. "Chin up! Think positively," he may say, to encourage his employees, peers, or superiors to function smoothly. Statements like "Follow that dream," and "Climb every mountain," sum up Interacting Socializer feelings. Though typically somewhat less motivated by change than Dominant Directors, Interacting Socializers become more susceptible to risk-taking when pressured by others to take the chance. If they haven't fully considered the ramifications, they may regret their impulsiveness after it's too late.

A classic Interacting Socializer who sought the U.S. Presidency was Hubert Horatio Humphrey, the charismatic Minnesota Senator. When he died, he received a stately funeral with more attention and sympathy than many whom had won the Presidency. Without such triumph, he moved the hearts of the entire nation.

What do Interacting Socializers want at work?

Interacting Socializers want companionship and social recognition, so their contributions to group morale often satisfy these needs. At work, they like to know everybody's first name and something about everyone. They can benefit from feedback from their co-workers, especially those who represent other behavioral types. Just as Steady Relaters contribute stability, Cautious Thinkers seek accuracy, and Dominant Directors add decisiveness, Interacting Socializers give their enthusiasm and energy. Tactfully reminding and assisting them so they will prioritize and organize can help the entire office function more smoothly. Since Interacting Socializers tend to be *open books*, the other types can detect when they are having an off day and give them a boost with a compliment or two.

As true extroverts, Interacting Socializers typically look outside themselves to renew their energies. They enjoy motivating books, tapes, and speeches—pick-me-ups that recharge their batteries to help them overcome obstacles. These are viewed as practical growth opportunities. They even prefer the terms *opportunity* or *challenge* instead of *problem*. A problem is too mired in negativism to comfortably fit with an Interacting Socializer's optimistic nature.

They prefer the "big picture"

As inductive thinkers, Interacting Socializers naturally think first about the big picture, then of supporting details. After seeing the broad overview, they prefer not to personally dwell on specifics. "Collins can work out the details." Interacting Socializers are intuitive and may naturally come up with assorted ideas—some practical, some not—but if they *feel right* to them, they *talk up* those ideas to others to elicit their feedback and enthusiasm. This can also serve the purpose of pulling Interacting Socializers back to reality if they venture too far out into *La-La Land* (one Dominant Director's description of this behavior at its most extreme). "Earth to Fred, earth to Fred!" may get an Interacting Socializer who's become too carried away back on course by using one of his own techniques—humor.

Interacting Socializers think aloud

Since Interacting Socializers like to talk more than average —to others and to themselves—they're likely to say inappropriate things more often than most of the other types. When talkativeness and emotionality mix, then hoof-in-mouth problems may set in with this behavioral type. Learning when to stop talking and start listening can help Interacting Socializers grow. Sometimes their naturally impulsive behaviors energize us; at other times their spontaneity requires more restraint.

They're idea people who throw ideas out. "Hal, we could do this (and this, or this, etc.)." This impulsive habit can get them in trouble. Why?

Because other people may think a commitment has been made, but the Interacting Socializer may not view the situation in the same way. Two weeks later, Hal may say, "Okay, I've done my part. When can you start action on yours?"

"What part are you talking about? I never agreed to anything, Hal. I was just thinking out loud." In this Interacting Socializer's mind, they hadn't formed an agreement, just brainstormed. Realistically, this type is much better at generating ideas than implementing them.

Fire! Fire! Fire!

Interacting Socializers can pump up their flexibility by better controlling their time and emotions and by developing a more objective mind set. They can benefit by spending more time checking, verifying, specifying, and organizing, or getting someone else to do it for them. Otherwise, Interacting Socializers may succumb to their excitable *Fire! Fire! Fire!* tendencies. If they concentrate on the task and take a more logical approach, then they can improve their follow-through.

For instance, Interacting Socializers may have so many things going that they may forget to finish tasks by a deadline; or they procrastinate until the last minute because of their multiple priorities. Writing things down and prioritizing can help the Interacting Socializer remember when to do what

Remember...

INTERACTING SOCIALIZER BUSINESS CHARACTERISTICS

- Like to brainstorm and interact with colleagues and others
- Want freedom from control, details, or complexity
- Like to have the chance to influence or motivate others
- Like the feeling of being a key part of an exciting team
- Want to be included by others in important projects, activities, or events
- Get easily bored by routine and repetition
- May trust others without reservation—take others at their word and don't check for themselves
- Typically have short attention spans, so they do well with many short breaks

INTERACTING SOCIALIZER:

PREFERRED BUSINESS SITUATIONS

- Like to work participatively with others

- Need immediate feedback to get, or stay, on course

- Like to mingle with all levels of associates and call them by their first names

- Enjoy compliments about themselves and their accomplishments

- Seek stimulating environments that are friendly and favorable

- Motivated to work toward known, specific, quickly attainable incentives or external motivators (dislike pursuits that drag out over long time periods)

- Open to verbal or demonstrated guidance for transferring ideas into action

- Like to start projects and let others finish them with whom. They can benefit from handy pocket calendars that go everywhere with them. If you fit the M.O. of this type, you can forget about using some little corner of an envelope to write on. You're probably too impatient to rifle through piles of paperwork to find it later.

Steady Relater Behavior at Work

Preferred job situations

Secure positions and careers where they can specialize in some areas and be part of a team

- Financial services

- Social worker

- Family doctor/nurse

- Residential or community services

- Teacher

- Personal assistant/secretary

- Insurance agent

- Librarian

- Customer service representative

Stability motivates them

In business and in their personal lives, Steady Relaters take one day at a time and may consciously avoid gambles and uncertainties. They tend to respect traditions and often demonstrate loyalty to everyone else while they trek along. Because stability in the workplace motivates them, Steady Relaters are apt to have the most compatible of all working relationships with each of the four types. Steady Relaters have patience, staying power, and stick-to-it-ivity, so they commit themselves to making relationships work.

They are extremely uncomfortable with conflict. In the workplace, this type may notice how others complete their tasks, but typically say nothing negative about their observations (with the possible exception of a close friend or family member). Why? They don't want to make waves and they don't want to appear to be know-it-alls. Silently, Steady Relaters may think they're shouldering the lion's share of duties, but they generally won't tell the boss or fellow employees. They'll just continue performing their own work and make the best of it.

"Be prepared"

If they need to make a presentation, Steady Relaters will probably thoroughly prepare and organize their material in advance. Since they feel comfortable with proven methods, they like to carefully acquaint themselves with each step of a procedure so they can duplicate it later. When taken to an extreme, this adherence to following instructions and maintaining the status quo can limit their actions.

Since Steady Relaters wear well and favor step-by-step procedures, they're natural choices for assisting/tutoring others, maintaining existing performance levels, and organizing systems. They often enjoy helping set up or implement guidelines that allow others to be more organized. Remember that Steady Relaters are the ones who assemble all their equipment first, set up their tools, and begin to work only when everything is in place.

For instance, when she's ready to collate, Steady Relater Paula places all the pages in descending order on a table. Next, she places a stapler on one side of the desk, extra staples close to that, and finally a large enough opening near page one for the completed stacks. When everything is ready, she begins to work on the completion of this task. Many a Dominant Director and Interacting Socializer who initially rolled their eyeballs at what they viewed as a laborious preparation stage have later found themselves marveling at such assembly line efficiency. At this point, a sincere compliment on her work procedure might be both appropriate and welcome. "Paula, your collating technique is more efficient than I could have imagined, let alone be likely to do myself."

The typical Dominant Director may want to delegate and oversee such a procedure: "Paula, you can start without assembling all that paraphernalia, can't you?" But for Steady Relaters, that's not a comfortable approach because they're advocates of the *Be Prepared* and *Plan Ahead* schools of thought. An Interacting Socializer may tend to haphazardly set up such a collating area, possibly on the floor, and omit key items like extra staples or adequate copies of page 13. "Darn, I need to go to the closet again," or, "Oh, no! I'll have to run to the store for more paper." Both of these individuals can waste more time than they thought they'd save because they didn't prepare as well as the Steady Relater.

Both the personalized people factor and going along with established practices rate high with this type. So when problems bombard Steady Relaters, they try to solve them by helping or working with others, following tried and true procedures, or a combination of the two. If these tactics fail, they may quietly do nothing. Doing nothing may include higher absenteeism; when conflict and stress increase, Steady Relater tolerance may decrease.

"Are we ready yet?"

As with any trait, the Steady Relater's propensity for studying procedures and doing repetitive tasks can sometimes be taken to an extreme. For instance, the following anecdote about the Steady Relater type illustrates this point. After Michelangelo (a Cautious Thinker, our next type) completed the frescoes on the ceilings of the Sistine Chapel, the Pope asked him to draw up architectural plans for St. Peter's Cathedral. Since Michelangelo had passed his 80th birthday, he drew up the massive and complex plans in less than two years and then turned them over to his most promising apprentice—a Steady Relater. This slower moving cohort's approach to implementing these plans was to study them step by step, day after day, year after year, time and again. Finally—after 23 years—he was ready to direct his efforts to the actual building of this world famous cathedral.

Service is their business

Steady Relaters tend to gravitate toward relationships that provide them with security, stability, and large doses of routine; these positions satisfy some of their rather maternal or paternal needs. While we know that not all elementary school teachers are Steady Relaters, this behavioral type is inclined to pursue careers that fit their natural desire for repeated group and one-to-one people contact, preference for sameness, and the opportunity to help or support others. Personally, we've observed many Steady Relater preschool, elementary, and middle school teachers—especially among those employees reporting higher levels of job satisfaction.

Actions speak louder than words

Inherently modest and accommodating, Steady Relaters usually think their actions speak for themselves. While Dominant Directors and Interacting Socializers pat themselves on the backs, Steady Relaters tend to simply nod and listen. Inwardly, they may want to divulge a personal triumph, but they won't volunteer it. If someone asks them about it, fine. Or, better yet, an ally may pipe up about the Steady Relater's coup. Steady Relaters tend to adopt a *Me last, if there's time,* attitude. At work, this type may think he should get a promotion, but is likely to just wait for the boss to notice what a good job he's doing, rather than bring it to his supervisor's attention.

S leaders

Politically, Steady Relaters act approachable and down-to-earth. Consider President Dwight D. Eisenhower, who also served as NATO's Supreme Allied Commander during World War II. His Presidential campaign button said simply, "I like Ike!" a Steady Relater-like understatement if there ever was one. The man was probably one of our most popular Presidents ever. Voters warmed to his down-to-earth, *Aw, shucks* mannerisms and easygoing smile. But despite their likability, Steady Relaters naturally have difficulty taking tough stands.

Steady Relater military leaders go by the book—a manifestation of their deductive, convergent, left brain orientations. They are driven by a basic need to use predictable, steady actions to yield known, proven results. At the most extreme, their battle cry is *Ready! Ready! Ready!* In fact, they might still be getting ready when the enemy fires. Then they may react by saying to others in their group, "Hold the fort!" Or "Toe the line!" Or "What's the SOP (standard operating procedure) for us to follow in this kind of situation?"

Steady Relaters want to be part of the group

Since Steady Relaters seek security and inclusion with the group, they can contribute to the workplace with their natural planning skills, consistent pace, and their desire to fit in. Like Interacting Socializers, they favor work relationships on a casual, first name basis; but Steady Relaters generally prefer developing special, more in-depth friendships with selected co-workers than do their social butterfly, Interacting Socializer, counterparts. So while Interacting Socializers may talk to anyone who will listen, Steady Relaters prefer involvement with a closer group of confidants.

Steady Relaters also want stability, steadiness, and a calm atmosphere in the workplace. They contribute to harmony in the office, so they usually fit comfortably into the work environment, but they also often become overly dependent on using the same old methods over and over again. Sometimes these procedures include steps needed when they learned the procedure, but which can now be discarded. They may improve their work productivity by using shortcuts that eliminate extra labor. Dominant Directors and Interacting Socializers can often help them with this. And, when asked, Cautious Thinkers can generally demonstrate new ways to get things done through other processes.

Why change?

The Steady Relater is the optimistic realist among the four types. A pragmatist, he likes to do routine things with familiar people to maintain the same situation. He performs regularly and deliberately toward this end of holding onto or striving for continuity, peace, and orderliness. Changes and surprises make him uncomfortable because they alter the current formula. Instead, he prefers to refine existing practices.

"Modesty is the best policy"

Just as they may think their own job performance needs no self-promotion, they may think (not say) the same about others' work. "I wish John would stop boasting about what a wonderful job he does. He seems to spend half the day promoting himself, rather than doing the work that's already on his desk." They often figure that if the boss (or anyone else) doesn't see what's going on, they don't want to have to be the ones to confront others about this unpleasant reality.

Remember...

STEADY RELATER BUSINESS CHARACTERISTICS

- Need to know the order of procedures

- Operate well as members of a work group

- Motivated by usual, known, and proven practices

- Oriented toward more concrete, repeatable actions

- Want order and ability in the workplace

- Focus on how and when to do things

- Work in a steady and predictable manner

- Like a long-term relationship with their business place and their fellow employees

STEADY RELATER:

PREFERRED BUSINESS SITUATIONS

- Like to perform the same kinds of duties day after day (no matter what the importance of the type of work involved)

- Prefer to work cooperatively with others to achieve common results

- Dislike taking risks

- Enjoy working in a stable, steady, low-key environment that has a minimum of changes

- Like to know each step toward completing their duties

- Prefer to make decisions by group consensus or other accepted practices rather than by themselves

- Enjoy feeling like valued members of the work group

How do they know, unless they see it themselves?

Steady Relaters operate predominantly from a deductive perspective. Instead of naturally sensing (Dominant Director), or feeling (Interacting Socializer), Steady Relaters think about things: "I think that something is really troubling John. His eyes are bloodshot, he's short-tempered and edgy, and he's been getting to work about an hour late for two days in a row." Even their feelings about others seem to be based on their thoughts about them. This ties in with the Steady Relater's more concrete or literal orientation. He often needs to see something with his own eyes before he's sure about it.

Steady Relaters take the indirect route

As naturally interested listeners, Steady Relaters appreciate this same behavior from others. They like others who genuinely share a common interest in exchanging thoughts, feelings, and experiences. This sometimes takes some extra effort, however, because Steady Relaters tend to speak indirectly. They seldom come right out and say what's on their minds, especially if they think something may be amiss. For example, a Steady Relater may know that everyone thinks a certain employee isn't pulling his own weight or has brown-nosed his way to the executive suite. Yet when pressed on this situation, he's likely to respond, "I don't want to say anything. I'd rather you observe things for awhile and come to your own conclusions."

At Work with the Cautious Thinker

Preferred jobs

Careers in which they can strive for perfection, creativity, and completeness

- Forecasters (political, weather, etc.)

- Critics (film, history, literary, etc.)

- Engineers

- Research scientists

- Data analysts

- Accountants/auditors

- Artists/sculptors/architects

- Inventors

Process and perfection

They see themselves as problem solvers who like structure, concentrate on key details, and ask specific questions about identified factors. They're masters at following important, established directions and standards, while still meeting the need to control the process by their own actions. Process-oriented, Cautious Thinkers want to know why something works, since such insight allows them to determine for themselves the most logical way to achieve the expected results—from themselves and others.

In business, Cautious Thinkers are practical and realistic. They seek neither utopias nor quick fixes. Because of their low risk-taking tendencies, they may overplan when change becomes inevitable. They like working in those existing circumstances which promote quality in products or services. When possible, they prepare ahead of time for their projects and then work diligently to perfect them to the nth degree. Their thorough preparation is designed to minimize the probability of errors. They prefer finishing tasks before or on schedule without mistakes caused by last minute rushing and inadequate checking or review.

Cautious Thinkers rank second only to Steady Relaters in their pursuit of logic. They rely on reasoning to avoid mistakes, so they tend to check, recheck, and check again. But they may become mired down with data collection. Amassing facts and specifics, they are uncomfortable with giving opinions or partial information until they've exhausted all their resources. This can frustrate people who want to know what's going on now, the types with faster paces. Additionally, all that checking can result in a disruption of the workflow.

They can benefit from checking only the critical things rather than everything. This procedure allows them to sort out and control the important details, and still get things done well. They can hold onto their high standards without becoming bogged down in relatively trivial business details. Cautious Thinkers need to learn to accept that perfection is an impossible quest, worth the effort in some instances, but not in others.

Cautious Thinkers prefer the "right" way

When airline pilots prepare to fly a commercial plane, they have a checklist of safety points before take-off. Cautious Thinker pilots have been found to focus far more on the most critical factors, using the remaining time to review the less crucial ones. In their typical Cautious

Thinker style, they complete the checklist the *right* way, by checking known factors against unknown variables. By contrast, Dominant Director pilots have been known to delegate this duty to someone else. With this, they then see to it that the task gets done their way. Interacting Socializer pilots have been observed getting *off task* by talking to co-workers they see during this process. Then they may wait till the last minute, due to their difficulty in assessing the amount of time needed to complete such detailed tasks. Steady Relaters go through each point, in the listed order, completing it in a step-by-step way, but without the same rigorous attention paid to those most critical items that the Cautious Thinker pilot scrutinizes. Although all four types finish the checklist, they have completed this task quite differently—according to their different work styles—and with the possibility of different outcomes as a result of their different approaches to the same task.

Old questions, new answers

Whether or not this type opts for a scientific or artistic career, they often follow a scientific method or intuitive, logical progression to achieve their objectives. Because of their natural inclination to validate and improve upon accepted processes, Cautious Thinkers tend to generate the most native creativity of the four types. Consequently, they often find new ways of viewing old questions, concerns, and opportunities.

Many artists and inventors fall into the Cautious Thinker category, many leaning toward experimentation and the possibility of coming up with new answers. Just as Michelangelo's creative mind envisioned completed sculptures entrapped in a solid piece of marble, Leonardo da Vinci perfected the Mona Lisa's expression in such a manner that its meaning still evades contemporary experts. Similarly, Galileo's creativity formulated precisely detailed plans of "impossible" futuristic inventions.

C leaders

Cautious Thinker leaders range from Thomas Jefferson to Henry Cabot Lodge and Adlai Stevenson. Each was a private person who exhibited calm, cool, objective behaviors which detractors at times viewed as aloofness and insensitivity. President Woodrow Wilson, often dubbed by scholars as the most intellectual 20th century president, also predictably fits this Cautious temperament. A former university professor, Wilson established far-reaching policies and practices, some of which still exist today. An intense, though private and contemplative individual, he was known as a man who was far ahead of his time in his Think(er)ing. The press had a heyday with *Silent Cal*(vin) Coolidge and his typical one or two word comments that often amounted to a clipped yes or no.

Cautious Thinker military leaders may use planned, careful actions to achieve their desired results. They may instruct their troops, "Don't ever let your guard down," or, "CYA (Cover your anatomy)!" If under extreme pressure, Cautious Thinker leaders may tend toward the *Aim! Aim! Aim!* mind set. They just keep aiming until they think they'll make a perfect shot.

People may complicate things

Like Steady Relaters, Cautious Thinkers are basically more introverted individuals who seek solace and answers by turning inward. Cautious Thinkers' natural orientation is toward objects and away from people. From their perspective, people are unpredictable and complicate things. The more people added to the formula, the more chance of getting unpredictable results.

Cautious Thinkers often choose to work with colleagues who promote calmness and thoroughness in the office—often either other Cautious Thinkers or Steady Relaters. Since Cautious Thinkers seek perfection, the other two types may help them modify that quest into a more time-efficient procedure. Dominant Directors can contribute by helping to explain realistic deadlines and parameters, so Cautious Thinkers can build those time frames into his procedures. Interacting Socializers, too, can help them *lighten up* more at work and teach them that there is more to the workplace than working alone eight hours a day.

When encouraged to do so, Cautious Thinkers can share their rich supplies of information with small groups of co-workers who can benefit from their wealth of experience and knowledge. This can enhance the Cautious Thinker's status with colleagues and become a bridge toward building teamwork and mutual understanding. Sharing with others can also serve to lessen Cautious Thinkers' reservations and suspicions about associates or even encourage Cautious Thinkers to stand up for themselves against those very people they may prefer to avoid.

They can also participate in more coffee machine conversation that may just give them a better understanding of co-workers, and possibly, some work problems. Carrying on a dialogue with associates may even provide them with insights into themselves. For instance, someone may observe, "Harold, you're furrowing your brow again."

Cautious Thinker Harold replies, "I am? I wasn't aware that I was."

"Yes, you do that a lot. That's why I've never said more than 'hello' to you. I thought you were either deep in thought or worried about something."

"Thank you for bringing that to my attention," Harold says. "I'll monitor that from now on."

Since Cautious Thinkers want clarity and order, they can contribute a natural sense of thoroughness to their company. They usually don't care about knowing everyone's name in their department, but they may make it a point to find out who they think exhibits the same thoroughness and precision they themselves have: "What's the name of the artist who drew up the graphics for the Robinson account?"

When the going gets loud

Cautious Thinkers (prefer to) get going. When discussions and tempers become hot and heavy, "I want to get out of this place" may represent the Cautious Thinker viewpoint. Because they want peace and tranquillity, they avoid and reject hostility and outward expressions of aggression. At the extreme, they can numb themselves to conflict to such an extent that they may have difficulty tapping into their feelings . . . not only anger and hatred, but caring and love.

By learning to accept others' expressions of emotions, Cautious Thinkers can also learn to accept their own feelings. Ideally, if the Cautious Thinker can consciously raise his tolerance for aggression, he can then begin to increase his ability to successfully deal with it in a more open manner through mutual exchanges.

Cautious Thinkers take themselves seriously

Since Cautious Thinkers often detect many of life's complexities that escape the other types, they can become perfectionistic and worrisome, with both themselves and others. While this quality control aspect can be very positive, when taken to an extreme, associates may dismiss the Cautious Thinker's caution as *crying wolf*. When Cautious Thinkers are willing to bend their standards on small matters, co-workers are more likely to listen to them for the bigger issues.

In the NASA space shuttle disaster, for instance, engineers repeatedly emphasized the need for more research. But after a few delays, the public pressure became so great that the Challenger was launched prematurely. That time, pushing the researchers harder and faster resulted in tragedy. The message: Listen to Cautious Thinkers about the big things. At the least, both positive and negative sides will come to light; at the extreme, the bleakest results will be projected. In either case, unknown factors become more clearly defined. At the same time, the obstacles and resources required for success are identified. The Cautious Thinkers exploratory process results in moving closer to the more desired goal or state shared by all parties.

Remember...

CAUTIOUS THINKER BUSINESS CHARACTERISTICS
- Concerned with process; want to know how something works

- Intuitive and original; once they know the expected structure, they may invent their own structure, method, or model

- More interested in quality than quantity; prefer lower output to inferior results

- Want to be right, so they employ logical thinking process to avoid mistakes

- Over-attend to details, sometimes impeding progress with regular checking and rechecking

- Dislike changes and surprises

- Reject aggression

CAUTIOUS THINKER:

PREFERRED BUSINESS SITUATIONS
- Colleagues and superiors do not criticize their work or ideas

- Can set the quality control standards and check to see if they're properly implemented

- Work with complete data systems, or can formulate some themselves

- Superiors value correctness and let them know they are key workers in the organization

- Workplaces are organized and process-oriented, with a minimum of socializing

Chapter 6
Leadership Styles

Making this chapter meaningful to you

Picture a Dominant Director, Interacting Socializer, Steady Relater, and Cautious Thinker who manage you or whom you manage. As you read, bear in mind each of these particular people and specify what you can do to improve your relationships with them. Focus on each one's more productive traits as well as each one's less productive characteristics.

The essence of this leadership chapter is that all people have their own natural, preferred way, of doing things, including exerting influence over people and/or managing tasks or organizations. In this respect, Dominant Directors are the most observably directive in their style of leadership. On the other hand, Interacting Socializers are the most naturally supportive in the way they go about their efforts to influence others and manage situations.

By contrast, the remaining two behavioral types are more introverted by nature and less easily identifiable in their leadership practices. Steady Relaters are more like supportive Interacting Socializers. But Steady Relaters are secondarily concerned with being supportive to provide the expected service or accomplish the identified result. And finally, Cautious Thinkers are more similar to self-determined Dominant Directors.

The difference is that Cautious Thinkers are concerned with achieving their own desired standards in a way that does not cause further problems by rubbing other people the wrong way.

The Dominant Director Leaders

Move over and let them do their thing

They're like wild horses that don't like to run in rigid formation. But why hobble them if they're able to get blue ribbons in their own way? Or even start and develop their own herd? If you confine them, Dominant Directors may become harsh and stubborn; let them do their own thing and they may very well impress you. Agree on the goal and specify the boundaries of the playing field. Then get out of their way. This requires other people to ignore some of the Dominant Director's natural competitive spirit and, instead, focus this energy on a common goal for bettering the organization. Dominant Directors seek this sort of encouragement and feedback to function most effectively within the general framework of shared expectations. But don't expect them to follow every procedure to the letter.

How to develop Dominant Directors

When coaching a Dominant Director, he likes to learn the basic steps to quickly sift out what he wants. "I don't really plan to read this 200 page computer manual just to learn how to set up pages in three columns. Just teach me what I have to know so I can do that." In the interest of saving time, D's may try to find shortcuts, so show them the simplest, fastest route to get them to their stated destination.

The thought of reassuring someone or explaining something more than once smacks of frittering away precious moments that he'd rather spend on action and results. So he doesn't bother with details. Focus on the high points, please, like what is to be done by when. He wants to know only those details required to get a contraption to function so he can then turn to other important new opportunities—like making money, for instance. Instead of covering steps one through 24, he prefers hearing about key steps 1, 6, 12, and 24. Forcing him to sit through all 24 points seems like torture to a D. This lack of attention to details can result in his searching for new ways to streamline his routine jobs in getting his desired effects more readily.

Toward appropriate management

When Don Cipriano, the former number one worldwide salesperson for Performax International, conducted a session on Motivational Management in London many years ago, he said, "We manage people the way they need to be managed, not the way we want to manage." One manager, John, commented that concept really hit home because his high D (Dominant Director) behavior was creating some problems with his S (Steady Relater) and C (Cautious Thinker) staff. For four months, John ran his office according to the way his staff needed to be managed, but when a new employee began working in his department, John didn't have the same success he had with the others. One day, she made an appointment with John and told him, "If you'd stop wasting time providing all those details, I could get my work done." John had made the common mistake of being so used to managing just S and C behaviors that he failed to recognize the high D behavior of his new employee. John later said to Don Cipriano, "I fell into the same trap, managing everyone the same way."

What's this company's philosophy?

Similarly, when Dr. John Lee, a renowned time management expert, conducted workshops, he often asked, "What is the operating philosophy of your company?" He said presidents of organizations seem floored when they noticed the diversity of answers mentioned by their staff members. If a CEO doesn't verbalize, clarify, and gather input about what everyone is working toward, how can the company function smoothly?

Who's managing whom?

Managing Dominant Directors is no easy task because they want to manage you! You can squelch them or you can encourage them to take control of certain arenas. Why not work with the D's strengths by allowing him to take the reins, where qualified, on particular projects? His preference for change and innovation makes him the natural choice for new frontier programs where he can implement his own ideas. Make sure the Dominant Director understands he needs to check with you at specific intervals, or he may demonstrate the renegade syndrome—doing his own thing, without answering to anyone but himself.

Getting Dominant Directors to decide

Dominant Directors tend to make autonomous, no-nonsense decisions. If the decision will help them meet their goals, they go for it; if not, they'll typically say no. One of the few times this type will procrastinate in reaching a conclusion is when it will take too much time or effort to do the homework to determine the best alternative. You can prevent this procrastination by simply providing a brief analysis for each option you present to a Dominant Director.

Motivating Dominant Directors

Provide them with options and clearly describe the probabilities of success in achieving goals. "Ross, here are four possibilities for developing the Evans Estate. I've highlighted the key points for each suggestion, and included costs and time projections on the bottom of each one. The choice is yours."

Compared to the other types, Dominant Directors are more likely to thrive in pressure cooker situations. They naturally gravitate toward those power positions and career areas where they can take charge: executives, politicians, military officers, stockbrokers, and newspaper reporters. Think of win-at-any-cost tennis pros. When in doubt, they question the decisions made by the referee. For better or worse, they deal directly with the source. It's not how you play the game—it's winning! And winning, more than anything else, motivates this type.

Complimenting Dominant Directors

Mention their achievements, upward mobility, and leadership potential. Omit personal comments and focus on their track record. "Jones, you've exceeded our company goals every month for the past year and have put in more hours than anybody but the top officials here. The CEO has his eye on you for an upcoming vice-presidential slot."

Counseling Dominant Directors

Stick to the facts. Draw them out by talking about the desired results. Then discuss their concerns. Focus on tasks more than feelings. Ask them how they would solve the problem. "Anne, we've heard a few comments that need to be addressed. It seems that some of your employees don't feel appreciated for the extra hours they've been putting in for you on the Evans project. They say they've given up social engagements and worked 14-hour days to beat your deadline. How do you think we can bolster their morale?"

Correcting Dominant Directors

Describe what results are desired. Show them the gap between actual and desired. Suggest clearly the improvement that is needed and establish a time when they will get back to you. "We need to streamline communication around here so that one hand knows what the other is doing. Last month, we had two separate divisions calling on the same CEO for corporate donations. I want you to work up a plan to keep everybody informed of who's working on what so we don't duplicate our efforts. Get back to me by the end of the week."

Communicating with Dominant Directors

Be prepared to listen to their suggestions, the course of action they have in mind, and/or the general results they are considering. This enables you to begin on a positive note by indicating the areas in which you already agree. Then you can work backwards toward gaining agreement on the results you both want—and are willing to either mutually or independently allow the other to achieve. "Sarah, this format will give you the freedom to develop your branch your way and still allow Vern and Ellen to structure theirs another way . . . without sacrificing time or morale."

Making decisions and problem solving with Dominant Directors

They will want to provide their own initial view of the decision to be made or problem to be solved and the process they prefer to follow in reaching a clear-cut, preferably quickly chosen solution. "As I see it, you have the most experience in organizing seminars like this, Charles, so why don't you throw out a few ideas!" You can anticipate, where possible, and be open to summarizing the achievements you've made (or, possibly in a case like this, your lack of achievements in this area). "Hal, you flatter me, but I've never undertaken an international convention like this before. As for ideas, why don't we decide who wants to perform which function and then we can all do what we feel comfortable doing!" With this approach, you're more likely to reach mutual agreement with the least hassle for everyone concerned . . . yourself included.

When suggesting a different idea, opinion, or action to them, be sure to point out you are trying to work in ways that are acceptable to them—and also yourself. Focus on your desire to identify solutions that will also meet their expectations. Stress that you don't want to cause difficulties for either them or you. "Phil, instead of writing this report as it occurs to you and me, I'd rather write an outline first and then the report. I know it takes longer initially, but it saves time in the long run because the writing will be better organized and make more sense to the readers."

When acknowledging Dominant Directors

When it's appropriate to reward or reinforce their behaviors, focus on how pleased you are. Assume they are also pleased with achieving the desired outcome in that situation. Also mention how glad you are to be a part of that process working with them to make things better for both of you through cooperation. The bottom line? Each of you gets better results by combining your energies on a common targeted goal: "Phil, this report turned out much better with your wonderful anecdotes and asides. Now we have something that's interesting, clear, and well organized!"

Delegating with Dominant Directors

Give them the bottom line and then let them do their thing. So that they can be more efficient, give them parameters, guidelines, and deadlines. "We need to get that mall built a month sooner or we'll lose our shirts. Fourteen tenants are threatening to bail out of their contracts if we don't open in time for the holidays. Don't spend more than another $30,000, keep everything legal and out of the newspapers, and get back to me by Monday morning."

We know one Dominant Director who became visibly, though not consciously, agitated if anyone stayed in her office beyond 10 minutes. Her staff knew this, but anyone outside the office had no inkling until she began fidgeting and examining her stacks of paperwork, hoping the person would leave. One day, it dawned on her to delegate an *alarm clock* duty to her secretary. Then, whenever anyone stayed more than ten minutes, Mrs. Myers knocked on the door or buzzed her on the phone reminding her of the *next appointment*.

Catch people doing something right

If you happen to be a Dominant Director manager, use what you now know about behavioral types to make the workplace more productive. Try mentoring, training, or consulting as appropriate development practices, instead of criticizing or leaving them alone without guidance. Catch your employees doing things right and tell them about it. Ask employees for their feedback about policies, deadlines, and programs. Bouncing ideas off your co-workers can give you insights into how you can better motivate people to help you achieve your goals.

Action Plan . . .

WHEN YOU ARE THE DOMINANT DIRECTOR

- Allow others to do things without excessive or untimely interference

- Participate in the group without expecting always to be in command

- Modify the tendency to give orders to others

- Enlist others' input and support through participative, collaborative actions

- Give others credit when they deserve it

- Praise people for jobs well done

- Let colleagues and employees know that you realize it's only natural that you and others will make mistakes

- When delegating, give some authority along with the responsibility

WHEN OTHERS ARE DOMINANT DIRECTORS, HELP THEM LEARN TO:

- More realistically gauge risks

- Exercise more caution and deliberation before making decisions and coming to conclusions

- Follow pertinent rules, regulations, and expectations

- Recognize and solicit others' contributions, both as individuals and within a group

- Tell others the reasons for decisions

- Cultivate more attention/responsiveness to emotions

The Interacting Socializer Leader

Help them focus their abilities

With their energy and enthusiasm, Interacting Socializers can get so involved with so many different activities that they may accomplish goals with a flourish. Or, they may show flurries of activity, but not actually accomplish things in the most efficient way. Managers and co-workers can help channel that energy and enthusiasm with tactful reminders and hands-on assistance to help them prioritize and organize. Then, the entire office may function more smoothly. Since Interacting Socializers tend to be open books, the other types often can detect when Interacting Socializers are having off days and give them verbal boosts with a compliment and personal attention.

How to develop Interacting Socializers

When coaching Interacting Socializers, don't give them too much at once or they'll become overwhelmed. Skip as much of the detailed, boring stuff as possible. Get them involved. Interacting Socializers are typically kinesthetic, hands-on learners, so let them try by first getting a feel for what's involved, and then showing you what they understood so you can give them structured feedback. Frequently, this type wants to jump in and try before they're ready, or before they fully understand everything. Allow them to save face when they do something wrong, and heap on those compliments when they get it right!

Prioritizing with Interacting Socializers

Many Interacting Socializers find that sorting out priorities and solutions becomes very difficult when too many opportunities bombard them. When this happens, they may become uncharacteristically mute and immobilized . . . temporarily, of course. Other people can help by prioritizing items for Interacting Socializers to tackle. "This account needs attention sometime today, but I need your input on the Chase report in less than an hour." This approach enables him to separate his feelings from the facts at hand as well as other people's expectations. Ironically, when the Interacting Socializer's tasks become more organized, his anxiety level lessens—despite the fact that he bristles at the thought of organization. More importantly, since he can't be all things to all people, focusing and refocusing on what's most important, second most, etc., is essential to his well being.

Support Interacting Socializers' dreams

Interacting Socializers operate predominantly from a multiple-focus, right brain perspective. They see mental pictures first, then convert those pictures to words. Preferring main ideas and generalities, not details, they base decisions on their impulses, gut feelings, and others' recommendations and testimonials. For this behavioral type, emotions rule. "Something tells me that I should buy this stock." This doesn't mean that they never use logic or facts, but that feelings and emotions come first, thinking processes being factors that are the servants to their feeling state.

Get ready to act more enthusiastic with an Interacting Socializer. Show you're interested in him by letting him talk and by using more animation in your own gestures and voice. Illustrate your ideas with stories or mental pictures that relate to him and his goals. He likes to interact with people, so try not to hurry your discussion. Include opportunities for small talk and getting personally acquainted.

Interacting Socializers like to envision the big picture. Generally less motivated by many facts and details, they respond better to short overviews or capsule summaries of what you plan to cover. Attempt to develop some stimulating, enjoyable ideas together while focusing on supporting their opinions and dreams. Interacting Socializers turn off to people who douse their dreams. Then support their ideas while showing them how they can transfer their talk into actions.

If you disagree, try not to argue because they dislike conflict. You might not win an argument with them anyway because their strong suit is feelings and intuition. If trapped, they can twist people around through very clever manipulation of feelings with their usage of words and emotions. Try to explore alternate solutions, instead. When you reach an agreement, iron out the specific details concerning what, when, who, and how. Then document the agreement with them, since they tend to naturally forget such details.

Motivating Interacting Socializers

They like special packages and a little something extra to inspire them to go the whole nine yards. "Hawkins, if you can clinch the Babbitt account, I'll give you an extra week's vacation and take you and Sharon to the fanciest restaurant in town." Or, show them how they can look good in the eyes of others. "When you close your next order, that will be your tenth major success story this year. You can all but clinch the President's Productivity Award with your name engraved on a plaque next to the big boss himself."

Many businesses use yearly contests to motivate their employees. Interacting Socializers tend to sprint toward a quick win—for the first week or two. Then they may say to themselves, "Hey, I have a whole year to win this contest. Why am I working so hard now?" They may further get sidetracked by other things and do nothing more about it until a week before the contest ends. If they can get excited enough, they may win anyway, but the truth is they haven't worked toward the goal for 11 months. How can these types keep up their motivation? Since Interacting Socializers like constant rewards along the way, they may favor shorter contests with smaller payoffs, perhaps culminating in the *big one* when the year ends. One person even jokingly suggests, "How about an employee of the hour award?" Or, they may enlist other colleagues' assistance who are better at implementation than they are.

Complimenting Interacting Socializers

Pay direct personal compliments to them, as individuals when legitimately deserved. "You are a terrific person and a wonderful employee." Mention their charm, friendliness, creative ideas, persuasiveness, and/or appearance (or better yet, all of the above). While other types respond to more specific job-related comments, Interacting Socializers can mentally relive more global generalizations for weeks to come. "We are so lucky to have you with us, Dee. You're a real gem."

Counseling Interacting Socializers

Give them ample opportunity to talk about whatever may be bothering them. Pay attention to both facts and feelings, but put your primary emphasis on their feelings. Ask probing questions and involve them by asking how they could solve the challenge or difficulty. Sometimes, just airing their feelings and thoughts relieves tension for these individuals. Talking allows them to get something off their chests and can even become an end in itself, since their energy is largely influenced by the quality of their relationship with a person.

Correcting Interacting Socializers

When stress hits Interacting Socializers, they prefer looking the other way and searching for more positive, upbeat experiences. They avoid problems as long as they can. If the pressure persists, they tend to literally walk away from the problem. When this tactic fails, they may become emotionally candid in attempts to meet their needs. "I can't believe I let this happen, but I brought it all on myself." Sometimes stress manifests itself in animated panic. "I can't talk now, Hal. It's really hit the fan this time!"

Let these individuals know specifically what the challenge happens to be. Define the behavior that can eliminate it and confirm the mutually agreeable action plan in writing to prevent future misunderstandings. Since they prefer keeping the conversation light, avoid what they view as negative or distasteful approaches. Rather than, "Why did your sales drop off 50% last month?" use more optimistically stated questions like, "How'd you like to bolster your sales up to your normal range and beyond it?" They'd simply rather deal with things going right.

Communicating with Interacting Socializers

Be prepared to listen to their personal feelings and experiences, since they have a need to be both expressive and able to share their emotions with others. Their style requires open and responsive interaction with others, preferably in a manner of congenial and unhurried conversation. It's much like that between long-time friends. "Just between you and me, Chris, I feel very uneasy about Jill and Howard handling this account by themselves."

Making decisions/solving problems with Interacting Socializers

They'll want to avoid a discussion of more complex, negative-sounding or otherwise messy problem situations. It's difficult for them to feel positive or agreeable with you or anyone else under these circumstances. In making decisions with them, they will be open to your suggestions—as long as these ideas will allow them to look and feel good—and not require a lot of difficult, follow-up, detail work or long-term commitments. "You know just about everybody who is anybody, George. Since we need to get $350 in pledges for the Y by the end of February, why not go ahead and wrap up all your calls by Friday. Then you can relax a lot more next week." When suggesting a different idea, opinion, or action to them, be sure to point out you are doing it that way if it's acceptable to them. Focus on your desire to identify solutions that will also meet their expectations. Stress that you don't want to cause difficulties for either them or you.

Above all, offer your suggestions as gifts which can make this situation (task or relationship) easier and more beneficial to them—as well as to other people who you feel are also likely to find this very acceptable and desirable. "You're lucky I'm on the Nominating Committee, Marilyn. So many people wanted the Hospitality position that I couldn't manage it for you this year, but I think I've got one that's even better than that—How about Junior High Dances?"

When acknowledging Interacting Socializers

When it's appropriate to reward or reinforce their behaviors, focus on how glad you are they have succeeded in finding a pleasant solution to their concern or objective. In addition, let them know how much you appreciate them for their openness and willingness to be responsive to you in a way that allows everyone to end up feeling good about the results afterwards. "George, I'm so glad we could reach a solution that both you and I feel good about. I appreciate your openness about only being able to call prospective donors on Friday night. That's fine with me. We'll work this out so that everyone is happy."

Delegating with Interacting Socializers

Again, make sure to receive clear agreement. Set up check points/times to avoid long stretches with no progress reports. Otherwise, Interacting Socializers may lapse into their natural way of doing things—spontaneously completing particulars which feel best while postponing less stimulating tasks, especially those that involve follow-up and checking.

By now, you realize that Interacting Socializers exhibit a natural talkativeness and ease with people. This makes them good choices for maintaining group morale and motivation. They think out loud and enjoy participating in brainstorming sessions anyway, so why not get their opinions and assistance on recognition awards, entertainment, or fund-raising activities? They want to fill their natural need by striving for recognition, so activities that draw attention to themselves appeal to them.

Interacting Socializers are often concept people who come up with plenty of ideas, but not necessarily the means of carrying them out, so steer them toward ways of assuring the implementation of those ideas. "Olivia, this proposal for the King Company looks good so far, but how about including more direct benefits for each employee. Marian has surveys filled out by each employee. Get together with her, bounce some ideas around, and then include more essential information about the eight or so key people in your proposal. Add some extra *plus points* on the others . . . 12 pages in all. In this manner, you should do the job very well. And, Olivia, thanks for making the extra effort on this project. It's really important to all of us."

In this example, the manager praises the work done so far, tells Olivia where to go for more facts, encourages a participative exchange between Olivia and Marian, spells out the parameters (12 pages), and shows her the path for staying on track. He's utilizing this Interacting Socializer's natural strengths and allowing for her potential weaknesses. Instead of delegating someone to perform large tasks that are naturally stressful for them, why not structure the tasks to fit the natural work style of that person? As one bumper sticker we spotted on a passing car advised, "Never teach a duck to sing. It's a waste of time and it annoys the duck."

Action Plan . . .

WHEN YOU ARE THE INTERACTING SOCIALIZER

- Attend to key details, when appropriate

- Improve your follow-through efforts

- Monitor socializing to keep it in balance with other aspects of life

- Write things down and work from a list, so you'll know what to do when

- Prioritize activities and focus on tasks in order of importance

- Become more organized and orderly in the way you do things

- Get the less appealing tasks of the day over with

- Pay more attention to time management of activities

- Check to make sure you're on course with known tasks or goals

WHEN OTHERS ARE INTERACTING SOCIALIZERS, HELP THEM LEARN TO:

- Prioritize and organize

- See tasks through to completion

- View people and tasks more objectively

- Avoid overuse of giving and taking advice (which can result in lack of focus on task)

- Write things down

The Steady Relater Leader

Encourage them to update their methods

Steady Relaters contribute stability and perseverance to their workplace. Since they work toward harmony in the office, they usually fit comfortably into the work environment, but they may become used to using the same old methods again and again. Sometimes their procedures include steps that may have been needed when they learned the procedure, but can now be discarded. They may improve their work practices by utilizing shortcuts that eliminate extra steps. Dominant Directors and Interacting Socializers can often help them with this. And, when asked, Cautious Thinkers can generally demonstrate new ways to get things done.

How to develop Steady Relaters

When he's in training for a job, he favors one-on-one, hands-on instruction with a real live human being, starting at the beginning and ending at the end. By learning each step, he generally is more comfortable with his functions. During training and in other newer situations, the S tends to observe others for a longer than average time. When he feels he can do a task, then and only then will he comfortably begin. This slower pace can frustrate Dominant Directors and Interacting Socializers, both of whom like to plunge right in with, "Oh, sure! I can do that," whether they've done it before or not! So understanding that Steady Relaters need to do things slowly can reassure the faster-paced types that the job will get done.

Get ready to be ready with the S. Have a step-by-step list of procedures or a working timetable/schedule at your disposal. Steady Relaters need to feel secure in their mastery of procedures until their actions become *second nature* and more routine. At the same time, they prefer a pleasant and patient approach while they learn what's expected of them.

Motivating Steady Relaters

Besides thinking they can learn to master a series of procedures, Steady Relaters like to also feel that their relationships with others can benefit from their follow-through. "If you can learn to use this computer by next week, you can send the whole Christmas mailing for Mr. Hawkins on Monday. Then he can go to Texas for his family reunion." Or show Steady Relaters how to strengthen their relationships with others. "When this office makes its 1000th sale, it can win the Outstanding Division Award for the year. And you, Arthur, can help that happen by getting Mr. Arens to look at this new demographic data."

- Focus on what's important now

- Avoid procrastination and/or hoping others will do things for them

- Practice and perfect, when appropriate

Complimenting Steady Relaters

Mention their teamwork and dependability. "Pam, besides plugging along on this project for two years, I really appreciate the fact you've encouraged everyone else to do their part. We couldn't have done it without you." Or remark about how others regard them, how well they get along with co-workers, and how important their relationship-building efforts have been to the company. "Limbrecht, you've been the glue holding this place together for the last 20 years." Effusiveness can arouse the suspicions of Steady Relaters, so stick to praising what they've done rather than more abstract, personal attributes. Otherwise, their modesty and your vagueness may cause them to dismiss your comments.

Counseling Steady Relaters

Allow plenty of time to explore their thoughts and feelings so you can understand the emotional side of the situation. Steady Relaters usually express their feelings less directly, so draw them out through questioning and listening responses. Bear in mind this type tends to balk at sudden change, whether the change is good or bad. The key point is that their stability-motivated state is disrupted by the unknown. You can help reduce their fears by showing how specific changes will benefit them and their company. "Barbara, moving to Dallas will be an adjustment for all of us at first, but 80% of our staff has agreed to go. The company will move you and your family, sell your house, add more medical and dental benefits to your health plan, and give you a 10% bonus for loyal service. We like to take care. Do the unpleasant, as well as the *fun things* of our own, and you are a valuable, trusted employee. And besides, you'll still be with many of the same friends, co-workers, and the company you've always been with day in and day out."

Correcting Steady Relaters

Reassure them that you only want to correct a specific behavior. Steady Relaters tend to take things personally, so remove the something is wrong with you barrier as quickly as possible. Don't blame or judge the person; keep the conversation focused on the behavior and its appropriateness. If the problem involves a procedure, help them learn how to improve it. Point out in a non-threatening way what they're already doing right while also emphasizing what needs changing. "Norma, I admire your persistence on this proposal, but we have to add more details to The Idea section before we send it out. For example…"

Communicating with Steady Relaters

Be ready to do more talking than listening with them, since they don't naturally feel comfortable when the limelight is focused on them. You will want to clarify any key agenda item with them, working to stay organized and moving forward steadily but slowly as you check to make sure they both understand and accept what is being said: "Did you want me to stick around the office at a particular time each day in case you need to telephone me for emergency questions on this account, or do you want me to call you?"

Making decisions and solving problems with Steady Relaters

In dealing with problems and decisions with this type, make sure to deal with only one subject or situation at a time, one step at a time. To gain clarity, before moving on to other items, make sure they are ready, willing, and able to do so. Recalling that they need stability, deal with matters calmly and in a more relaxed manner. Encourage them to share their suggestions as to how the decision might be made in a way that is likely to add even more stability to the current conditions than already, or previously, exist. "Would you mind writing down a schedule of your office's activities so I can get my proposal written up without missing anything? "

When suggesting a different possibility to Steady Relaters, point out how you are trying to identify ways that you can help continue to make things pleasant for them. You simply have an idea or opinion in this respect which will also help stabilize your own relationship expectations with them and which is important to you, too. "I know that we initially agreed on 10 phone calls per day, but some of our volunteers are unable to make that commitment. Would you be comfortable making 15 calls a day if those calls included your personal friends and family?"

When acknowledging Steady Relaters

When it's appropriate to reward or reinforce their behaviors, focus on how you genuinely and sincerely appreciate their willingness to work to make things good for you and others. Approach matters in a more systematic, low-keyed, and understandable manner. Also, point out how you have noticed they make important contributions when they take the initiative to share their own ideas, interests, and insights in helping make sure these results are achieved. "Just say anything about the impending merger that you want to share. We certainly don't want to use any high-pressure tactics, which is precisely why you meet our own expectations so well. John, thank you very much for your willingness to provide us with this desired input."

Delegating with Steady Relaters

Steady Relaters may be reluctant to ask others to do their own share of the work. So you could make a personal appeal to their loyalty and sense of sportsmanship. "Al, you're an example for this company of genuine cooperative spirit. Your staff wants to please you, so by giving everyone in your department just 10 of those names to call, you can all reach the goal together by noon tomorrow. Otherwise, you'll probably have a lot more difficulty reaching all those people by the target date." Give them the task, state the deadlines that need to be met, and explain why it's important to do it that way. "I'll need 500 copies of these summaries typed and collated by 5 p.m. today. Mr. Jeffries is getting back from New York two days early and he wants them by tomorrow morning."

Action Plan ...

WHEN YOU ARE THE STEADY RELATER

- Stretch by taking on a bit more (or different) duties beyond your comfort level

- Increase verbalization of your thoughts and feelings

- Speed up your actions by getting into some projects more quickly

- Desensitize yourselves somewhat, so that you aren't negatively affected by your colleagues' feelings to the point of affecting your own performance

- Learn to adapt more quickly to either changes or refinements of existing practices

- Bolster your assertiveness techniques

WHEN OTHERS ARE STEADY RELATERS,HELP THEM:

- Utilize shortcuts and discard unnecessary steps

- Track their growth

- Avoid doing things the same way

- Focus on the goal without attending to other thoughts or feelings

- Realize there is more than one approach to tasks

- Become more open to some risks and changes

- To feel sincerely appreciated

- Speak up and voice their thoughts and feelings

- Modify the tendency to do what others tell them

- Get and accept credit and praise, when appropriate

The Cautious Thinker Leader

Help them substitute quality for perfection

Since this type is characterized by the most complex thinking pattern, they base their decisions on proven information and track records. They want to make rational choices based on facts, not on other people's opinions or testimonials —unless those people are those Cautious Thinkers' personal heroes.

Even then, they'll probably want to see it in writing. When a C says, "I need to think about it," she usually means it. You can help her make a decision by supplying the materials she requests and by allowing her the time to make the right decision for her. Focus on emphasizing deadlines and parameters so the Cautious Thinker can build those time frames into her procedures.

How to develop Cautious Thinkers

When coaching a C, point out the most important things to remember first. Then demonstrate the procedure in an efficient, logical manner, stressing the purpose of each step. Proceed at a relatively slow pace, stopping at each key place in the process to check for his or her understanding. Ask for possible input, especially regarding desired refinements that may be appropriate. This approach ensures success with the task and minimization of stress for the Cautious Thinker.

Motivating Cautious Thinkers

Appeal to their need for accuracy and logic. This type doesn't respond well to fancy verbal antics, so keep your approach clear, clean, and documentable. Better yet, provide illustration and documentation. Avoid exaggeration and vagueness. Show them how this is the best available current option. "Ms. Alberts, our office cleaning service should meet almost all your cleanliness needs. I think that a neat and sanitary environment is a key standard for more productivity. Do you agree or see it differently?"

If they decide to take part in a competitive situation, they'll probably do it as they do other tasks—bit by bit—until they do it right. Unlike their colleagues who may show enthusiasm at the beginning, Cautious Thinkers often show the patience and follow-through to ultimately win—if they perceive the contest as worthwhile and don't become too preoccupied with details along the way. Whereas some people focus on winning shorter-term battles, the Cautious Thinker is motivated by the ultimate sense of lasting personal glory derived from triumphing in the overall war.

Complimenting Cautious Thinkers

Mention their efficiency, thought processes, organization, persistence, and accuracy. Don't mix personal and professional comments unless you know them very well. Even then, they prefer more privately communicated, plausible praise. "Jeffries, you were so thorough on this project that we had every shred of information we needed—and then some just in case we required a safety net. Thanks again for another good job!"

One C told us, "Compliments don't mean much to me. I really don't think about them. But I do like genuine, heartfelt appreciation once in awhile, like, "You did a fine job," or, "I've really benefited from your work and so have others who have told me about your contributions." In other words, keep praise simple and concise for a Cautious Thinker. He went on to say that what he thinks about some accomplishment is much more important to him. "I'm hard on myself."

Counseling Cautious Thinkers

Elicit their thoughts about processes, procedures or problems, perhaps by asking something like, "If it were in your power, how would you change this to make things even better?" Like Steady Relaters, they often express their thoughts and opinions indirectly, so persist in your attempts to get them to talk. This type dislikes change because they typically view changes and the future as unknown variables where unforeseen mistakes might happen. They need to plan for change ahead of time so they can identify and bring under control any key considerations that have to be addressed in the process. When possible, allow them to investigate possible repercussions, especially at the beginning stages. That way they'll know more about the future and may be more comfortable with possible changes.

Correcting Cautious Thinkers

Show Cautious Thinkers the way to get a job done and they'll typically master the format, then modify it to suit their individual needs. They tend to start with what they have to work with, then personalize it, almost from the beginning, so that it works better as they see it. So they may avoid people whom they perceive might tell them to do things differently. This is one way Cautious Thinkers maintain control of their work. They tend to side-step authorities who they think are endeavoring to correct them. At the extreme, this behavior can appear sneaky to other types, especially if the C gets caught.

Specify the exact behavior that is indicated and outline how you would like to see it changed. Establish agreed-upon checkpoints and times. Allow them to save face, as they fear being wrong. "Nelson, your work here is typically done neat, on time, and right on the money. Now that we're switching the office to computers, you'll be able to turn out the same quality of work, only faster. I'd like you to take this computer class..."

Communicating with Cautious Thinkers

Be well organized and clear in your communications, since they are likely to ask lots of questions about a situation or subject in their search for a logical conclusion. You may want to have them clarify what their more pressing key concerns are. Ask your questions in a more discreet, non-judgmental manner to elicit the points, objectives, or assurances Cautious Thinkers want. "Lenny, I'm not trying to pressure you, but are you not interested in the auditor's position, or in any position?"

Making decisions and solving problems with Cautious Thinkers

Set the stage by making sure they are open to discussing the problem or decision being considered at this time. If they aren't ready, either set a definite time that's better for both of you or explore their concern in even pursuing this subject. When the situation is being explored, review your impression of the entire process. "My understanding is this—you'd like to think it over for a week or so and figure out what kind of time commitment you'd be able to make to the group. When may I call you about your decision?" Decide on a logical approach for gaining common agreement about both the nature of the problem or decision involved and the most reasonable way of finding how to resolve it. Do so in a way that is likely to be most satisfactory to them, you, and any other key individuals involved.

When suggesting a different possibility to Cautious Thinkers, point out how you would like to be able to identify those ideas, perspectives, or actions likely to allow you, them, and others to reach a more perfected solution or situation. Stress how less difficulties or confusion are likely to result. Ask them what insights and suggestions they, or individuals they know and value, could bring to this situation. "Carol, if we leave at 10 o'clock Friday morning and get to Palm Springs around 11:00, we can meet with Mr. Conkill and his VPs for lunch to present our ideas for organizing their grand opening party. Do you know any wholesalers we can contact there so we can come up with a realistic estimate for making their party a bona fide hit?"

When acknowledging Cautious Thinkers

Focus on your realization of how difficult it can be at times for them to attempt to meet the high personal standards they set for themselves. Also focus on how much you appreciate this personal characteristic for what it's done to make things better for you in your relationship with them. Cite a specific and appropriate example that proves this point. "Robert, you're a very good chef. That salmon was cooked perfectly— juicy and flavorful without a hint of dryness. I don't want to embarrass you, but I feel obliged to share with you how truly impressed I am. Thank you for your efforts." Then, notice his reaction. If it's discomfort, share with him that you did not mean to embarrass him, but just to let him know how much you value him. If his reaction is more positive, ask him to tell you more about the sense of satisfaction and enjoyment he derives from similar things. "I'll bet you like creating other recipes, too. Is that correct?"

Delegating with Cautious Thinkers

Take time to answer their most critical questions about structure and/or guidance they require in a specific situation. The more they understand the details, the more likely they will be to complete the task properly. Be sure to establish deadlines. "Angela, the court date on the Mortimer case has been moved up to Monday, so we have to respond by speeding things up a bit. It will proceed almost as efficiently as if you researched everything by yourself if we enlist two associates to help you work, under your direction, on tasks you delegate to them and then review. Before getting started, do you have any preferences on the *who's* or *how to's* of this process that you think are essential to check with me at this time?"

Action Plan . . .

WHEN YOU ARE THE CAUTIOUS THINKER

- Modify criticism (whether spoken or unspoken) of others' work

- Check less often, or only check the critical things (as opposed to everything), allowing the flow of the process to continue

- Ease up on controlling emotions; engage in more water cooler interaction

- Accept the fact that you can have high standards without expecting perfection

- Occasionally confront a colleague (or boss) with whom you disagree, instead of avoiding or ignoring them (and doing what you want to do, anyway)

- Tone down the tendency to OVER-prepare

WHEN OTHERS ARE CAUTIOUS THINKERS, GENTLY REMIND THEM TO:

- Share their knowledge and expertise with others

- Stand up for themselves with the people they prefer to avoid

- Shoot for realistic deadlines and parameters

- View people and tasks less seriously and critically

- Balance their lives with both interaction and tasks

- Keep on course with tasks, with less checking

- Maintain high expectations for high priority items, not necessarily everything

The "best" leadership style

Remember that there is no such thing as one best, all-purpose leadership style. Instead, the best leaders are those who realize what a job, role, or specific situation requires for successful performance and then ensures those outcomes. At times, this may involve a clear-cut match between your own strengths and the required actions. At other times, behavior requirements may vary. The effective leader may adapt his own natural style by using new behavior methods he has learned. Or he might call upon other qualified individuals whose talents and energies can more productively handle the immediate problem. Or a good leader may take action to modify the environment. This could include shifting the work priorities to ensure the successful completion of the necessary task without sacrificing the well being of other people. Using these breakthrough leadership techniques and options will maximize productivity.

Chapter 7
Selling and Servicing with Style!

Every sales or service call has certain similarities; however, the techniques differentiate the professional salesperson from other salespeople. Professionals focus more on helping than selling, more on listening than talking, more on problem solving than persuading, more on creating long-term customers than one-shot sales.

The techniques used by professionals are simple, yet powerful. Salespeople who use this approach concentrate on a consultative process that allows both the customer and the salesperson to feel good about the sales/service exchange and each other. Professional sales and service staff go through five specific steps, though the approach may vary, depending on the behavioral style of their prospects.

You can apply the tips in this chapter to help you maximize your sales and service encounters, whether you fill the role of buyer or seller. Think of someone you know in a sales or service situation who sounds like the Dominant Director, Interacting Socializer, Steady Relater, and Cautious Thinker. How can you benefit with each one of them in a business relationship?

Step #1—making contact

The purpose of talking with your prospect is to begin building a business relationship by opening up lines of communication. Professional salespeople know that a solid business association goes beyond the immediate product or service being offered. The relationship, and therefore, the sale, requires the establishment of trust and the building of credibility. When prospects know you sincerely have their best interests in mind, the rest of the process can continue. Today's buyers are appreciative of professionals who show an interest in them, their businesses, and their lives.

Step #2—studying needs

Professional sales and service people spend a great deal of time studying their prospects' needs. They look not only for needs but also for opportunities. Searching just for needs implies customers just have problems that must be solved. Looking for or creating opportunities puts the salesperson in the position of a consultant who can take someone's current conditions and improve upon them. They can encourage the prospect to become involved in this exploratory process. By asking well-structured questions, offering thought-provoking possibilities, and studying the many facets of the prospect's situation, you build cooperation—and a foundation for shared commitment.

Step #3—proposing solutions

After meeting with the potential customer and studying his or her situation, the next step is to propose a solution to the problem. The professional approach is one in which the presentation is custom tailored to the prospect's needs. Because of the comprehensive discussions the service or salesperson has had with the prospect, benefits naturally emerge as they relate to specific problems.

Step #4—gaining commitment

This is a logical conclusion to the ongoing communication and agreement that has been taking place with the prospect. Since the salesperson and prospect have worked together on a common goal since the beginning, there are few reasons why objections would be voiced at this point. There may be details to work out, but they won't get in the way. For professional sales and service people, the confirmation becomes a question of when, not if. If resistance occurs, it simply indicates there is a need for gathering more information or clarifying some details. Gaps in communication are not a problem because experienced salespeople are willing to spend time with the prospect until everything is understood and acceptable.

Step #5—assuring satisfaction

Professional sales and service people thrive on satisfied customers and see them for what they are—assets! These veterans begin assuring customer satisfaction after the sale by changing hats from salespeople to quality service providers. They make sure the customer receives the proper order on the right delivery date. They also help the customer track the results and analyze the effectiveness of the product or service for the specific problem(s) addressed. By assuring the satisfaction of each customer, professionals build a clientele guaranteeing future business that will become annuities for life.

How to Sell Your Product or Service to Dominant Directors

Dominant Directors want to know the bottom line. "What will this do for me?" and "By when?" Just give them enough information to satisfy their need to know about overall performance. They don't want you wasting their time reconstructing your product bolt by bolt, giving a laundry list of testimonials about your other satisfied clients, or getting too chummy with them. Even if you don't consider yourself a salesperson, remember that everyone sells something every day—whether ideas, integrity, credentials, etc. Regardless of your work, you can probably apply to your everyday life a few sales tips that typically work with Dominant Directors.

#1—making contact with the D

When you write, call, or meet a Dominant Director, do it in a formal, businesslike manner. Get right to the point. Focus quickly on the task. Refer to bottom line results, increased efficiency, saved time, return on investment, profits, and so on. In other words, tell him what's in it for him.

If you plan to sell something or present a proposal to a Dominant Director, take care to be well organized, time-conscious, efficient, and businesslike. As impatient as they are with a slower pace, Dominant Directors become especially wary if they question a person's competence. Make sure they don't question yours. Remember, Dominant Directors don't want to make friends with you; they want to get something out of you if they think you have something to offer. And they're usually willing to pay for it.

As a sales or service person, it is your job to provide both sufficient information and enough incentive for the Dominant Director to meet with you. When you call, you might say, "Some of the ways I thought we would be able to work together are X, Y, and Z. Could we discuss those when I call you at a time of your choice?" By planting a seed, you may raise his interest level and the priority of your next call, unless, of course, he just isn't interested. Since individuals who fit this type pride themselves in being busy, they dislike granting several meetings. But if they think that time spent now will save time later, they're likely to initially explore matters with you now, rather than later.

#2—studying D's needs

To head off the Dominant Director's impatience before it surfaces, keep your queries interesting by alternately asking questions and giving additional information. Do this in a practical manner. Dominant Directors need to view the meeting as purposeful, so they want to understand where your questions ultimately lead. When asking a Dominant Director questions, it is essential to fine-tune and make them as practical and logical as possible. Aim questions at the heart of the issue and ask them in a straightforward manner. Only request information that is unavailable elsewhere.

When gathering information, ask questions showing you have done your homework about their desired results and current efforts. Know the Dominant Director's industry and company. Be sure to make queries that allow him to talk about his business goals. "Since your leadership has brought your company from 27th to 3rd in the country, what happens now?" Gear your studying toward saving the Dominant Director time.

#3—proposing solutions for D's

Your presentation, whether it is combined with studying or given on its own, must be geared toward the Dominant Director's priorities. He is concerned with saving time, generating money, and making life easier and more efficient. If you gear your presentation toward how he can become more successful, you'll no doubt get his attention. Zero in on the bottom line with quick benefit statements.

Because of their lack of time, Dominant Directors do not focus as much energy on contemplating and evaluating ideas. They want you to do the analysis and lay it out for them to approve or disapprove. Dominant Directors like rapid, concise analyses of their needs and your solutions.

So how can a salesperson get into a better business relationship with a Dominant Director? Be prepared. In addition, demonstrate your competence and show him how your product will help him achieve his goals. Focus on results and highlight important specifics. Cut out intermediate steps when you make your presentation, eliminate the small talk, and stick to business. Professionalism counts with the Dominant Director.

During those times when it's appropriate to give historical data about your company or a more detailed presentation, write it out before you call. This allows you to highlight key points with a marking pen before you see him. Otherwise you're liable to bury him in a mass of paperwork. Skip over less important facts and show him the bottom line basics. Then leave a copy of the printout with him so he can refresh his memory later. Or he may want to delegate the fact checking to someone who really enjoys it—a Cautious Thinker or Steady Relater.

There's another good reason for reviewing your material, printing it out, and highlighting it. A Dominant Director may fire off questions at what seems to be a faster-than-the-speed-of-mouth rate. When he wants to hear about how your product ties into the bottom line, he wants to know now. Determine if he really needs the information immediately to make his decision or if he just wants to challenge you. In many cases, if he gets the information an hour from now, you can still meet his needs.

#4—gaining commitment with the D

With Dominant Directors, you can come right out and ask whether they're interested. You might say, "Based on what we've just discussed, are you interested in starting our service or carrying our product?" A Dominant Director will often tell you yes or no in no uncertain terms. At times, though, this type can put you off as if they can't make a decision, when, in fact, they aren't even thinking about it. They can become so preoccupied with other business that they literally do not have the time to evaluate your ideas, especially if they don't have enough information.

When you draw up a commitment letter, pay attention to how much time you spend on points the Dominant Director may not care about. Explain your commitment to attain both his bottom line results and your goals for a mutually acceptable agreement.

Consequently, the best way to deal with a Dominant Director is to give him options and probable outcomes. Bear in mind that the Dominant Director likes to balance quality with cost considerations, so include this information when you want him to make a decision. Then offer options with supporting evidence and leave the final decision to him. "The way I see it, you can go with Option A (tell pros and cons), Option B (more pros and cons), or Option C (still more pros and cons). I've outlined these three plans, costs of implementation, and approximate completion dates. Which one sounds best to you?" Dominant Directors seek control, so let them make the final decision. Brief and to the point, like the D himself, this approach automatically fills his need to have the final word.

#5—assuring D satisfaction

Since Dominant Directors usually don't emphasize a personal relationship in business, if you sell to one, don't rely on past sales to ensure future purchases. Follow up with the Dominant Director to find if he has any complaints or problems with your product. If he does, fix them or his impatience may motivate him to seek help elsewhere, probably with another company. As Willy Loman found out in *Death of a Salesman*, contacts meant nothing in an age that emphasized change and product performance.

Impress upon your prospect that you intend to stand behind your product or service. Further, stress that you will follow up without taking a lot of his time. "You're buying this to save effort and time. I want to make sure it continues to work for you. I'll periodically check back to make sure everything is running smoothly, but I don't want to waste your time with unnecessary calls. When I telephone, if everything is fine, just say so and that will be it. If anything is less than what you expect, I want you to call me right away and I'll see to it the problem is fixed immediately." You may also want to offer a money back guarantee "If you aren't satisfied that you got your money's worth, I will personally take back the merchandise and write you a check."

SALES AND SERVICE STRATEGIES FOR DEALING WITH DOMINANT DIRECTORS:

- Plan to be prepared, organized, fast-paced, and always to the point

- Meet them in a professional and businesslike manner

- Learn and study their goals and objectives—what they want to accomplish, how they currently are motivated to do things, and what they'd like to change

- Suggest solutions with clearly defined and agreed upon consequences as well as rewards that relate specifically to their goals

- Get to the point

- Provide options and let them make the decision, when possible

- Let them know that you don't intend to waste their time

How to Sell Your Product or Service to Interacting Socializers

As with the other types, apply your active listening skills, but be an especially empathic listener with Interacting Socializers. Give positive feedback to let them know that you understand and can relate to what they're feeling. When you talk about yourself, remember to use feeling words instead of thinking words. To paraphrase this concept, share your vision of the world in terms of your emotions, opinions, and intuitions. Tell stories about yourself, especially humorous or unusual ones, to win the heart (and sale) of an Interacting Socializer. Allow them to feel comfortable by also listening to their stories, even to the point of talking about topics that may stray from the subject.

#1—making contact with the I

When you write to or personally meet an Interacting Socializer, give the letter or meeting an upbeat, friendly feeling and faster pace. Don't talk about features, specifics, or performance data. In your initial benefits statement, stress those aspects of your product or service that will give them what they want—status, recognition, excitement, and being the first one on their block to have the newest, most dynamic product or service you can offer.

The first time you call an Interacting Socializer, use a more open-ended, friendly approach. Tell him who you are and say something like, "I'd like to come by and show you an exciting new product that will analyze and organize your accounts and help you become even more of a top performing salesperson."

When you meet an Interacting Socializer, think (or more specifically, feel) in terms of someone running for election. Shake hands firmly, introduce yourself with confidence, and immediately show interest in him personally. Let him set the pace and direction of the conversation.

Since Interacting Socializers typically enjoy talking about themselves, ask questions about them. "How did you got into this business?" Prepare for lengthy answers, though. Plan to have as many meetings with an Interacting Socializer as necessary to build the relationship and gather information. After your first visit, you may want to meet for breakfast or lunch. Placing a time limit on those two meals is easier than putting a cap on dinner.

#2—studying I's needs

Interacting Socializers get bored quickly when they're not talking about themselves. That's why so much information gathering needs to revolve around them. But remember to strike a balance between listening to their life's stories and gathering the information you need to be an effective sales consultant. When asking business questions, keep them brief. If you can, work these exploratory questions in with the social questions. "You mentioned people as one of the keys to your success. How do you find (recruit) the people you work with? What kind of training do you give them?" The better your relationship with an Interacting Socializer, the more willing he'll be to cooperate and talk about the task at hand.

Interacting Socializers can be so open they may tell you their fondest hopes and aspirations. If you can demonstrate how your product or service can get them closer to their dreams, they may become so excited about your product—and you—that they're likely to sell themselves to you.

#3—proposing solutions for I's

Style is as important as substance, so sell the sizzle as well as the steak. The presentation should show an Interacting Socializer how your product or service will increase his prestige, image, or recognition. Talk about the favorable impact or consequences your suggestions will have in making their working relationships more enjoyable. Give them incentives for completing tasks by stressing how their contribution will benefit others and evoke positive responses from them. Presentations need impact for this type, so involve as many senses as possible. Interacting Socializers want both the presentation and the product to feel great. They also want to be reminded of who else has it; but spare them the details of other people's successes. Show them how you can save them effort and still make them look good.

Back up your claims with testimonials from well-known people or corporations. Interacting Socializers respond well to other people's positive experiences with your product or service—so tell them who else uses it. If one of their heroes tries something, they're likely to try it, too. Better yet, name some satisfied acquaintances that the Interacting Socializer knows and admires. He may even respond with, "Go no further. If it's good enough for Frederick Mullens, it's good enough for me. He probably spent weeks researching, comparing, and contrasting. He really knows what he's doing. You should put that guy on your payroll."

#4—gaining commitment with the I

Be open and ask, "Where do we go from here?" or, "What's our next step?" If your inventory is low, tell them. "I see you really are excited about this. I only have three left. Do you want one now?" Interacting Socializers are very spontaneous and respond well to the bandwagon approach "Everybody's doing it." If they like something, they buy it (all other things being equal). You may have to hold them back because they also tend to overbuy, a behavior that both you and your customer may live to regret.

Interacting Socializers don't like paperwork and details, so they're likely to hesitate, and even procrastinate, when it comes to spending the time required to create a commitment letter specifying who does what by when. "Do you really think I won't live up to my word?" While a handshake is usually good enough for them, you'd be wise to have a written understanding. Both of you may hear the same words, but Interacting Socializers tend to interpret those words in a positive light—and often to their advantage. For this reason, it may help to draw up a summary in advance and go over it with this type of prospect. Make absolutely sure that you agree on the specifics or, later on, you can almost bet on some degree of misunderstanding and disappointment.

When the Interacting Socializer tells you a written agreement isn't necessary, simply say that you need such a clear summary for your own benefit so as to help yourself and others remember what is expected. Also mention that you appreciate their show of faith in you. You might say something like, "I just want to make sure that we're in 100% agreement, Mark. I'll feel better about this if I keep a record for us to have if we ever need to refer to it in the future." When you put your concerns in terms of such desired positive feelings, how can the Interacting Socializer object?

"Okay, if it will make you feel better about it, but I'm already 100% sure," he may respond. Next, if required, change whatever details require changing and the job will be done, quickly and painlessly. Finally, go ahead and write up this agreement as a means of verification and send or, better yet, give him a copy in person. Then you'll have a much better shot at a more long-standing, productive business relationship.

#5—assuring I satisfaction

In business, as in love, Interacting Socializers frequently buy before they're sold. When they jump in too quickly, the probability that they may suffer buyers' remorse is higher than for the other behavioral types. Interacting Socializers need ongoing reminders that they've made the right purchase decision because they get bored quickly, even with new things. So make sure you reinforce their decision by giving them plenty of service and/or assistance immediately after the sale. Be certain they actually do use your product, or this type may get frustrated from incorrect usage and either put it away "never to be used again"—or return it for a refund.

Think of yourself as an organizer for a basically less organized type to allow them to get the most out of your product. As a bonus for the extra effort, remember that they tend to *talk up* or *talk down* whatever pops into their minds. Since they mingle with so many people, you can even ask them if they would be willing to share with others their glowing testimonials about you and your product or service.

SALES AND SERVICE STRATEGIES FOR DEALING WITH INTERACTING SOCIALIZERS:

- Show that you're interested in them, let them talk, and allow your animation and enthusiasm to emerge

- Take the initiative by introducing yourself in a friendly and informal manner and be open to new topics which seem to interest them

- Support their dreams and goals

- Illustrate your ideas with stories and emotional descriptions that they can relate to their goals or interests

- Clearly summarize details and direct these towards mutually agreeable objectives and action steps

- Provide incentives to encourage

- Quicker decisions

- Give them testimonials

How to Sell Your Product or Service to Steady Relaters

Steady Relaters, concerned with maintaining stability for themselves, want to know step-by-step procedures that are likely to meet their need for details and logical follow-through action. Organize your presentation—list specifics, show sequences, and provide data. If possible, outline your proposals or materials. Satisfy their need to know the facts, but also elicit their personal feelings and emotions by asking for their input on "how to" aspects.

Listen patiently to Steady Relaters, projecting your true interest in them as individuals in their own right. Express your appreciation for their steadiness, dependability, and cooperative teamwork. Get to know Steady Relaters personally. Flex yourself to be non-threatening, pleasant, friendly, but still professional. Develop trust, credibility, and friendship at a relatively slow, informal pace. Then communicate with them in a consistent manner on as regular a basis as is required.

#1—making contact with the S

Contacts with to Steady Relaters are best when soft, pleasant, and specific. Include the human element as well as references to things. Mention the name of the person who referred you. "Hello, Mr. Newhouse, I'm Sheldon Doolittle with the Pinpoint Acupuncture Clinic. Mary Walsh said you would appreciate knowing about me and my clinic. Oh, she did call you? Good. If you'd like, I could come by, we could get to know each other, and I can tell you about the ways other people have relieved their allergies with our treatments." Remember that you may have the best product or service in the world, but if the Steady Relater doesn't like you, she'll settle for second, or even fourth best, from a salesperson she likes.

#2—studying S needs

Steady Relaters can be excellent interviewees. Talk warmly and informally and ask gentle, open questions that draw them out, especially around more sensitive areas. Show tact and sincerity in probing about their needs. "Mr. Harmon, I noticed that you've been here for 30 years. You must have seen a lot. Hypothetically speaking, how would you go about refining a few of the things that aren't working around here in the Information Systems Department?"

If they do not have a good feeling about your product, company, or even you, they will not take the chance of hurting your feelings by telling you so. They want to avoid confrontations, even minor ones. So Steady Relaters may tell you what they think you like to hear, rather than what they really think. This same reticence may apply to telling you about their dissatisfaction with your competitors. Even though this is exactly what you want to hear, the Steady Relater may think, "I know it hasn't been working well, but they're such nice people. I don't want to say anything negative about them."

#3—proposing solutions for S's

Show how your product/service will stabilize, simplify, or support their procedures and relationships. Clearly define their roles and goals in your suggestions, and include specific expectations of them in your plan. Present new ideas or variations from their current routines in a non-threatening way. Provide them with the time and opportunities to adjust to changes in operating procedures and relationships. When change becomes necessary, tell them why. Explain how long the changes will take and any interim alterations of the current conditions. Design your message to impart a sense of stability and security. "This plan will enable you to continue doing things the same basic way, with a few updates here and there. Don't worry about the updates because I'll be here to walk you through them each step of the way. And the real benefit, in the final analysis, is that this refinement will result in more stability than we now have."

Concentrate on security, harmony, steadiness, and concrete benefits. "This pension plan could help your entire staff save for their retirement with a minimum amount of worry. Even though Social Security may be tapped out by the time they retire, they'll be able to depend on this safety net." Answer their concerns about how and what as well as you can. Reassure them that you'll find out about the information they want to know; then do it. Stress that this isn't a big change, just a way to help them do what they already do . . . only better.

Steady Relaters like to be shown the appropriate steps to follow, so share those with them. "After you turn the equipment on, push the blue button to activate the computer. When you hear the motor, begin." Involve them by asking their opinions. "Is this an important concern for you, or are you looking for some other specific benefit, instead?"

#4—gaining commitment with the S

Steady Relaters are slow, deductive decision-makers. They listen to the opinions of others and take the time to solicit those opinions before making up their minds. So make a specific action plan. Provide personal guidance, direction, or assurance as required for pursuing the safest, most logical course to follow. When you reach agreement, try to explore any potential areas of misunderstanding or dissatisfaction. Steady Relaters like guarantees that new actions will involve a minimum risk to their desired stable state, so offer assurances of support.

Try not to rush them, but do provide gentle, helpful nudges to help them decide, when needed. Otherwise, they may postpone their decisions. Involve them by personalizing the plan and showing how it will directly impact them and their co-workers. "Our system will identify which employees deserve immediate raises at a faster rate than our old method." When asking for a commitment, guide them toward a choice if they seem indecisive. "We've gone over all the possibilities for improving customer service, Seymour. I think this option is the best because it will generate the most customer interest. Why don't we go ahead and implement it now?"

Another approach is to lead Steady Relaters. Once you have determined which action is in their best interest, lead them to the confirmation with your recommendation. "Jean, we've talked about a lot of things and I firmly believe this is the best solution for you. I would not recommend it if I wasn't 100% convinced it will work for you." When you've gained agreement, you can gently lead the Steady Relater to the next step. "If you agree with everything we've just discussed, our next typical step with a customer is to fill out the agreement and then begin the process with a deposit."

There is nothing pushy or manipulative about this if you have studied your prospect's needs and are now recommending a solution that you honestly believe best satisfies their needs. Then it's a win-win situation. Anything less is actually a losing proposition for this prospect.

#5—assuring S's satisfaction

Practice consistent and predictable follow-up. Give them your personal guarantee that you will remain in touch, keep things running smoothly, and be available on an as needed basis. Steady Relaters like to think they have a special relationship with you, that you are more than just another business acquaintance. Remember they dislike one-shot deals, so follow up to maintain your relationship. Of all the types, they most prefer a continuing, predictable relationship. Impersonal, computerized follow-through is not as appealing to this type, so continue building your business relationship with your low-keyed attention and offers of assistance. "I'll call on you once each month to make sure you're satisfied with our product. If you have any problems or concerns at all, just phone me at my office and I'll get back to you as soon as I can. In fact, here's my home number."

SALES AND SERVICE STRATEGIES FOR DEALING WITH STEADY RELATERS:

- Get to know them more personally and approach them in a non-threatening, pleasant, and friendly ... but professional . . . way

- Develop trust, friendship, and credibility at a relatively slow pace

- Ask them to identify their own emotional needs as well as their task or business expectations

- Get them involved by focusing on the human element . . . that is, how something affects them and their relationships with others

- Avoid rushing them and give them personal, concrete assurances, when appropriate

- Communicate with them in a consistent manner on a regular basis

How to Sell a Product or Service to Cautious Thinkers

Cautious Thinkers are precision people, efficiency experts who want to do their jobs as they want to do nearly everything else: the correct way. They also seek confirmation that they're right, but won't typically volunteer that need. Going about tasks slowly so they have enough time to check things out, they dislike rushing or being rushed. They operate on a level that prefers thinking words, not feeling ones, so build your credibility by remembering to think with your head, not with your emotions. Focus on their level of understanding about the what's and why's of your proposal.

#1—making contact with the C

Before meeting, tell them briefly what you'll cover so they know what to expect. This can be done when you make the appointment. Show them logical proof from reliable sources that accurately documents your quality, track record, and value. Once you've verified your credentials, preferably in writing or with tangible examples (make copies of a few), you can establish your product's or service's credentials, too.

Speak slowly. Economize on words. Explain why you are contacting them. This type doesn't care as much about social interaction, beyond courtesy and pleasantness, so get to the point. Avoid making small talk and speaking about yourself, except to initially establish your credibility. Cautious Thinkers tend to be somewhat humble and are naturally suspicious of those who talk themselves up.

#2—studying C needs

Cautious Thinkers often like to answer questions that reveal their expertise, so they can be very good interviewees. As long as you ask logical, fact-oriented, relevant questions, they tend to enjoy talking to you. Phrase your questions to help them give you the right information. "How many pages of completed copy do you typically write per week?" Ask open and closed questions that investigate their knowledge, systems, objectives, and objections. "When do you foresee finishing this project?" or "What possible problems do you think you might encounter?" Let them show you how much they know.

Make your own answers short and crisp. If you don't know the answer to something, don't fake it. Tell them you'll get the answer for them by a certain time, then do it.

#3—proposing solutions for C's

Emphasize logic, accuracy, value, quality, and reliability. Present obvious disadvantages. Make your points, and then ask if they want further clarification. They dislike talk that isn't backed up with both supporting evidence and achievement-focused action. Describe the process that you plan to follow. Then outline how that process will produce the results they seek. Elicit specific feedback. "So far, what are your reactions? Do you have any reservations that you'd like to clear up?" (They probably do, so encourage communication.) "Specifically, how do you view the practicality of applying this computer program to satisfy your current requirements?"

Of all the types, this one is the most likely to see the drawbacks, so point out the negatives before they do. Such honesty will only enhance your credibility. If you don't draw attention to the disadvantages, this type may view your failure to do so as a cover-up. Instead, let them assess the relative costs versus benefits that are typical trade-offs when making realistic choices between available, competing, yet imperfect, products or services.

#4—gaining commitment with the C

Provide logical options with documentation. Give them enough time and data to analyze their options. Unlike Dominant Directors and Interacting Socializers, this type is uncomfortable with snap decisions. When they say they'll think about it, they're probably serious. On the other hand, when a Steady Relater says, "I'll think about it," he may be stalling, or may, in fact, not want your product.

Unless Cautious Thinkers have already researched the field and determined that your product is the best, they probably have your competitors calling on them. Know your competition so you can point out your advantages relative to what they offer. This type is the most likely to do their own comparative shopping, so mention your company's strengths as you suggest questions they may want to ask your competitors. "Ask them if they have an unconditional money-back guarantee," or, "How long have you been in business?" or, "Will they also train new employees at no additional cost?" In short, point out the things your company does as well or better than your competition. Do this in a factual, professional way that is based on allowing them to do a comparative *cost-benefit* analysis of the options.

#5—assuring C customer satisfaction

Set a specific timetable for when you'll measure success. Continue proving your reliability, quality, and value. Make yourself available for follow-up on customer satisfaction. "Mr. Quimby, I'll check back with you on Tuesday morning, if that's all right, to make sure that your new phone system is functioning correctly. Here's my card with the numbers of my office, home, and emergency 24-hour hotline if you experience any problems."

SALES AND SERVICE STRATEGIES FOR DEALING WITH CAUTIOUS THINKERS:

- Prepare, so that you can answer as many of their questions as soon as possible

- Greet them cordially, but proceed quickly to the task; don't start with personal or social talk

- Hone your skills in practicality and logic

- Ask questions that reveal a clear direction and that fit into the overall scheme of things

- Document how and why something applies

- Give them time to think; avoid pushing them into a hasty decision

- Tell them both the pros and cons and the complete story

- Follow through and deliver what you promise

Afterword

After reading *People Smart*, we hope that you will apply what you have learned to enrich all aspects of your life from your workplace to the social arena, including family experiences and romantic encounters.

You now have the tools to create relationships that are more positive for yourself and others.

Mutual respect and commitment are the keys to understanding and getting along with people. Of course, degrees of respect and commitment vary from relationship to relationship. You probably do not feel as committed to your grocer or butcher as you do to your spouse, significant other, or best friend. However, using what you now know about People Smart concepts, you can learn to accept and even appreciate the differences in others.

Remember that people's strengths can be carried to the extreme at times. You can actually encourage them to act in ways that are more positive by consulting the appropriate charts and graphics in Chapters 5-7.

Identify the person's behavioral style by using the inventory in Chapter 2, identify the environment, and then use the visuals to help you enhance your relationship with that person.

If you want to identify your own personal behavioral style online, go to http://www.DISCstyles.com/assessmentorder.asp

You get an in-depth, personalized 29-page DISCstyles report; 30 days of free, unlimited Observer Assessments; and a weekly ezine providing you both descriptive and prescriptive lessons on how to be People Smart in all your interpersonal interactions.

Now, a Word About Our Authors...

Anthony J. Alessandra, Ph.D.

Dr. Tony Alessandra helps companies build customers, relationships, and the bottom line. Companies learn how to achieve market dominance through specific strategies designed to outmarket, outsell, and outservice the competition.

Dr. Alessandra has a street-wise, college-smart perspective on business, having fought his way out of NYC to eventually realize success as a graduate professor of marketing, entrepreneur, business author, and keynote speaker. He earned his **BBA** from the University of Notre Dame, an **MBA** from the University of Connecticut and **PhD in Marketing** from Georgia State University.

Dr. Alessandra is founder and president of AssessmentBusinessCenter.com, a company that offers online multi-rater assessments and tests; co-founder of **MentorU.com**, an online e-learning company; and Chairman of the Board of **BrainX**, a company that offers online digital accelerated-learning programs.

Dr. Alessandra is a widely published author with 14 books translated into 17 foreign languages, including **Charisma** (Warner Books, 1998); **The Platinum Rule** (Warner Books, 1996); **Collaborative Selling** (John Wiley & Sons, 1993); and **Communicating at Work** (Fireside/Simon & Schuster, 1993). He is featured in over 50 audio/video programs and films, including **Relationship Strategies** (American Media); **The Dynamics of Effective Listening** (Nightingale-Conant); and **Non-Manipulative Selling** (Walt Disney).

Recognized by *Meetings & Conventions Magazine* as "one of America's most electrifying speakers," Dr. Alessandra was inducted into the Speakers Hall of Fame in 1985, and is a member of the Speakers Roundtable, a group of 20 of the world's top professional speakers. Tony's polished style, powerful message, and proven ability as a consummate business strategist consistently earns rave reviews.

Contact: Dr. Tony Alessandra, Alessandra & Associates. Inc., 5927 Balfour Court, Suite 103, Carlsbad, CA 92008 Phone: 1-800-222-4383 or 1-702-567-9965 Fax: 1-760-603-8010 email: TA@Alessandra.com Website: www.Alessandra.com <http://www.Alessandra.com>

Michael J. O'Connor, Ph.D.

Dr. Michael O'Connor is an accomplished author, consultant, business advisor, speaker and trainer. He has three decades of experience working with both private and public companies and organizations of all sizes both domestically and internationally. He continues to work daily with organizations, groups and individuals to build their current and future success. The nature of his continuing contribution is reflected in the reputation he has gained as "the consultant's consultant" and "executive's coach."

He has authored over two hundred products that are used for the assessment and development of businesses, leaders and employees, and work groups. These include instruments, training programs, hands-on diagnostic tools, audio and videotapes, and computerized materials/services. Dr. O'Connor is also currently the co-author of six books. In their historical order of authorship these are: Mysteries of Motivation, People Smart, People Smarts, The Platinum Rule, Managing By Values, and Developing Leadership & Character.

Dr. O'Connor has formerly been a university professor, served as Vice President for Consulting & Resources Development at the Carlson Learning Company and been a senior external consultant to the Hay Group of Companies for its European Sector. His clients have ranged from the largest to small, family-owned businesses. Some of the recognizable client names include IBM, Shell, AT&T, United Airlines, Citibank, Chase Manhattan Bank, Florida Power & Light, Airlines Reporting Corporation and numerous U.S. Government Agencies and the American Management Association.

He is Managing Director of the Center For Managing By Values and continues to actively lead his own business, Life Associates Inc. **Contact:** Dr. Michael O'Connor, Life Associates, Inc., 3461 Bonita Bay Blvd., Suite 111, Bonita Springs, Fl. 34134, Phone: 941 947 1111, Fax:941 947 3311, Email: drmoconnor@lifeassociatesinc.com

Janice Van Dyke, Ph.D.

Janice VanDyke, Ph.D., has written dozens of articles that have appeared in various national trade journals.

CLAIM YOUR BONUS: PeopleSmart Six Hour Audio Program on Downloadable MP3s

Imagine...

- When you encounter difficult people - you know how to adapt to them.

- Where you meet challenging situations - you have the skills transform them.

- In times when you face the unknown - you remain fearless.

Imagine having a instantly downloadable product that will teach you to master the above skills that you can burn to a CD, put on your MP3 player, or access on your laptop or PC...

If you dream of all of that and more... Then PeopleSmart is the MP3 series you need. is a unique blend of scientific research on human behavior and my 30-plus years of teaching people smarts - through the Platinum Rule.

The PeopleSmart MP3 series is a unique blend of scientific research on human behavior and my 30-plus years of teaching people smarts using the Platinum Rule.

Once you've been exposed to these hands-on, proven and practical principles, you'll find that you will have access to uncommon wisdom allowing you to:

• Become a more loved and effective boss

• Gain effortless cooperation of even the most difficult people

• Fascinate and influence your spouse and children

• Build quick rapport that creates life long relationships

• Get along with all types of people from every walk of life

Curious about how PeopleSmart achieves all this?

Well, here's its secret formula...

Ever wondered why your natural behavior sometimes seems to alienate people?

It is because that same behavior may not be natural for others. You know in your heart - you have the highest intentions. If you want to get along with your colleagues, employees, bosses, friends, and family, it's essential to become aware of your natural tendencies - and their natural preferences!

Here is the key...

You must learn to determine and distinguish the four major behavioral styles.

PeopleSmart shows you how do this, by helping you to learn about your own style first, then showing you quick and easy ways to identify the styles of others. Finally, you learn how to adjust your behavior so that you become versatile, adaptable and widely popular.

It gets even better.

Learn to apply PeopleSmart and soon you unconsciously begin to draw out the best in everyone around you. You notice how easy it becomes for you to gain the trust and respect of even the most cynical people you meet.

The PeopleSmart MP3 series is very enjoyable to listen to and simple to apply.

Download yours today at
www.Alessandra.com/peoplesmart

Here is just a fraction of what I cover in these six power-packed MP3s:

• How to treat others the way they want to be treated, not the way you want to be treated - without being phony or underhanded.

• A description of each behavioral style to help you determine which one you are.

• How to identify other people's styles.

• How to get along with everyone at work, school, home - anyone and anywhere.

This is a listener-friendly MP3 series. You can use and reuse it as a constant companion to consult when dealing with difficult people and stressful situations.

PeopleSmart gives you the tools to get what you want in various personal and work situations and equips you with the power and knowledge to cash in on these insights through more positive and productive exchanges with others.

You can realistically take charge of improving all your work relationships and this MP3 series tells you how.

Additional Learning Tools:

DISCstyles

An indisputable fact is that people prefer to interact with people they like. The ability to create rapport with people is a fundamental skill in sales, management, personal relationships, and everyday life. The goal of DISCstyles is to create personal chemistry and productive relationships. You do not have to change your personality. You simply have to understand what drives people and recognize your options for effectively dealing with them.

DISCstyles teaches you powerful life-skills that will serve you well in all your relationships: business, social and family.

To FULLY EXPERIENCE THE MAGIC OF DISCstyles, TAKE YOUR DISCstyles ASSESSMENT NOW.

http://www.DISCself.com/?mj

Dynamics of Effective Listening - *Six Hour Audio Program on downloadable MP3s*

Active Listening Skills: What they didn't teach you in school could be the key to becoming closer to your friends and family; a better, stronger leader; and finally able to explode your earning potential.

Active listening is a skill so important that anyone who lacks it is sure to have problems at home and at work: problems with a spouse, kids, customers, a boss (or bosses), or co-workers. When you don't know how to listen to others, you can't help but create misunderstandings that end up costing a lot of time and money. But those trends do not have to continue.

The Dynamics of Effective Listening is an MP3 audio program that will teach you how to effectively listen to others. Dr. Tony Alessandra and his thirty plus years of researching human behavior will help you tap into your own communication power. You can master the skill of active listening in just a few short weeks.

BUY IT NOW! http://www.alessandra.com/products/productdetails. asp?productid=77

Astounding Customer Service *80 - minute Audio Program on downloadable MP3s*

Download this 80-minute MP3 series right now and you're moments away from acquiring the most critical and valuable skill that could mean thousands (maybe more) to your bottom-line.

How much is a valued customer really worth to your business? Do the math. It costs you up to 4 times more to get a new customer than it does to retain an existing one.

BUT WAIT...

That doesn't even take into account the fact that an unhappy customer will tell an average of 20 customers about their bad experiences, while a satisfied customer will only tell 10 people about their good experiences.

This means you have to make twice as many customers happy as unhappy - just to break even!

Call me stupid but I'm keeping my customers happy and satisfied... and the only way to do it is through Astounding Customer Service!

Download this 80-minute MP3 series right now on your computer and you're moments away from acquiring the most critical and valuable skill that could mean thousands (maybe more) to your bottom-line.

I've laid it all out for you here - over 35 years of the customer service secrets that have helped me tremendously in my own business career and saved me from many ruined customer relationships along the way.

BUY IT NOW! http://www.alessandra.com/products/productdetails. asp?productid=78

How to Gain Power and Influence with People - *5 1/2 Hour Audio Program on downloadable MP3s*

WHEN YOU HAVE THIS, YOU NEVER HAVE TO ASK TWICE!

Ever meet someone who made you feel small in his or her presence? Like they could see right through you, size you up, and get you to do pretty much anything they wanted?

It's a very strange feeling, believe me. You feel like you're being pulled in by a tractor beam. You desperately want to resist and despise this person. It could be a salesperson, your boss, even a relative. But you can't because they are just so darn charming and persuasive.

WHAT'S THE BIG SECRET?

Well, as an applied behavioral scientist and human relationships expert, I have spent my entire career studying this mysterious effect and what I learned really surprised me...

There's no secret! What we commonly think of as the mystical, magical power of persuasion and influence is really just a set of practiced techniques any eleven-year old could follow.

In fact, if you had an hour today you could learn these cut and dry techniques for yourself and use them immediately on the people in your life to get them following immediately in line with your agenda!

HERE'S HOW TO DO THAT:

My research revealed some specific qualities that all powerful and influential people demonstrate. I used this research to create a system to help you and people like you strengthen their Power and Influence muscles.

The system is called How to Gain Power and Influence WITH People MP3 audio album.

AND YOU CAN DOWNLOAD IT INSTANTLY!

This is 5 1/2 hours of pure fascination. Listen to it for just an hour and you will gain Power and Influence that will help you:

• Get far more respect than the average person does

• Be admired and adored, seemingly without effort

• Exude huge amounts of self-confidence and self-esteem

• Appear extremely powerful without being intimidating

• Easily get what you want, because people instinctively want to help you

WITH THIS SYSTEM YOU GET 12 POWER AND INFLUENCE-BUILDING SESSIONS, COVERING:

Session 1-The Power of Charisma

Session 2-Maximizing Your Personal Power

Session 3-Making a Powerful First Impression

Session 4-Power Energy and the Aura of Success

Session 5-The Power of Because

Session 6-The Power of Space and Time

Session 7-Power Speaking

Session 8-Power Listening

Session 9-The Power of Personality

Session 10-Power Rapport

Session 11-Power Adaptability

Session 12-Testing Your Power and Influence

BUY IT NOW! http://www.alessandra.com/products/productdetails. asp?productid=79

Mastering Your Message - *5 Hour Audio Program on downloadable MP3s*

Learn to communicate like a Boardroom Warrior!

• Do you ever feel like half the room is asleep during your presentations?

• Do you worry that your company meetings aren't productive - that people are leaving more unclear about things than when they came in?

• Are you frustrated with being overlooked, of not having an impact, of having a great idea but not knowing how to voice it?

• Are you self-conscious of the way you stand and speak - are you concerned that your body language may be sabotaging your career?

• When employee conflicts erupt, do you resolve them quickly, or do you add fuel to the fire by being tentative and non-direct?

This program will help you take your first steps on the path to becoming a masterful communicator, a wizard of interpersonal exchange, a Boardroom Warrior. Order my mp3, Mastering Your Message today, and experience for yourself the increase in personal power I am promising. You can download the entire program in less than 2 minutes by clicking on the link below. Within 45 minutes of listening to the very first volume, you'll be able to walk into work tomorrow like a changed person. (Your office will see it too!)

BUY IT NOW! http://www.alessandra.com/products/productdetails. asp?productid=80

Simplicity - *Five Hour Audio Program on downloadable MP3s*

Lead a Happy, Balanced Life with Jeff Davidson and Tony Alessandra's "Simplicity" 12-Chapter MP3 Set:

YOUR SANITY MAY DEPEND ON IT!

When you are finally able to implement Simplicity in your life, that is, cut out the complexities that swallow your time and raise your stress level, you will notice that you'll have more time and energy to dedicate to strengthening the bonds with those that matter most. Stop juggling and learn how to live a happy, healthy, productive, stress-free, and well-balanced life. That's right, it's as simple as that. Now you can learn how to have it all too!

BUY IT NOW! http://www.alessandra.com/products/productdetails. asp?productid=81

Alessandra on The Power of Listening *downloadable MP3*

Sharpen Your "Business Radar" In Just 60 Minutes!

• Do you forget important information the second you leave a meeting with a client, co-worker, or boss?

• Do you have a difficult time really focusing in on what the other person is saying without letting your own thoughts and pre-judgments get in the way?

• Are you missing out on the "silent messages" people are sending you through body language and gestures?

• Would you like to give yourself an edge in negotiations, picking up on the "subtle" clues of conflict and frustration other people miss?

THEN UNLEASH THE POWER OF LISTENING!

Of all the business skills critical to your career and personal success, I rank powerful listening skills to be #1. Why? It's simple.

In case you haven't noticed, business today is about one thing: gathering information. The person who gathers the most "correct" information in the shortest period of time is most likely to make the correct judgments and the correct decisions. This is true for any position - from corporate executives to customer service!

If you're dealing with "cold" computer printouts and fact sheets all day, that's one thing. But if your job involves "warm" daily interaction with clients, customers, coworkers, and managers, then you know your primary tools for gathering this vital information will be your ability to "tune out" your own thoughts and distractions and completely "tune into" what the other person is saying. Both through their words and their body language.

BUT ARE YOUR TOOLS SHARP ENOUGH?

Unfortunately, most of us are pretty lousy listeners. In your average conservation, you're lucky if you can process and retain 10% of what the other person is saying. This has nothing to do with memory and everything to do with how skilled you are at organizing and compartmentalizing information in your brain as soon as it comes in.

Thankfully for you, I've created The Power of Listening. This is an entertaining and informative MP3 audio program you can download right now that teaches you all the vital tricks to increasing your listening abilities so you can learn more, observe more, and retain more from each and every one of your conversations.

Having this information at your fingertips is like having a hand-held high frequency radar you can pull out during meetings, client presentations, and everyday office interactions so that no vital information slips through the cracks. Not only can you process and remember more of what anyone says, but you'll be able to tell if what they're saying is actually the truth! Do their words match their actions? Is someone nervous, or are they open and calm? The Power of Listening teaches you!

BUY IT NOW! http://www.alessandra.com/products/productdetails. asp?productid=85

Alessandra on NonVerbal Communication
downloadable MP3

Be the Master of Your Unspoken Message

Have you ever allowed your eyelids to droop at a conference, made jarring hand motions in a boardroom meeting, delivered a podium address with weak vocal intonation... and not even been aware of it? Did you know that what you don't say can have a great affect on how everyone perceives you?

LIKEWISE, DO YOU KNOW WHAT TO LOOK FOR IN OTHERS' NONVERBAL MESSAGES?

For example, an employee enters your office, shoulders slouched, body rigid, and sits down with his arms and legs crossed. His lips perched and fists clenched, he avoids all eye contact and makes nervous, fidgeting gestures.

You give him the benefit of the doubt and believe what he says. However, if you knew the secrets of NonVerbal Communication, you could have read his body language and exposed him for lying.

KNOW FOR SURE BY LEARNING THE LANGUAGE OF NONVERBAL COMMUNICATION!

The way you communicate nonverbally is responsible for 90 percent of what people think of you. It's the difference between being considered weak or powerful, unsure or confident, insecure or ready to take on the world. You could use authoritative words, have excellent listening skills, or be an expert with feedback, but if you don't understand nonverbal communication, your communication and ability to detect what others are communicating is not as effective as it should be.

Knowing exactly what to look for in your own gestures and vocal intonations will help you communicate a powerful message, confidence, and an assured presence. On the flip side, having a keen eye for others' unspoken messages will enable you to know what they are really saying - before they open their mouths to speak.

ALESSANDRA ON NONVERBAL COMMUNICATION MP3 WILL HELP YOU GET IT RIGHT!

In just the one hour it takes to listen to my Alessandra On NonVerbal Communication MP3, you'll walk away knowing how to target yours and others' specific gestures, movements, vocal intonations - and decipher what they all mean. It really works. Once you understand this non-verbal language, you'll be able to use it to your advantage. The winner in you will consistently shine through, and no one will be able to fool you again.

BUY IT NOW! http://www.alessandra.com/products/productdetails. asp?productid=86

The Platinum Rule - *Two-Hour DVD*

Dr. Tony Alessandra delivers a LIVE program in front of several hundred business people in a Detroit theatre. You get nearly 75 dynamic minutes of The Platinum Rule topic and a BONUS of nearly 45 minutes on Customer Loyalty and Collaborative Selling on a single DVD. Lucky for you and me, there were two studio-quality cameras rolling that caught every word, every laugh, and every nugget-of-wisdom Tony had to share that day. Now you can laugh as you learn how to gain instant rapport and get along with nearly anybody you meet no matter who they are.

That day, Dr. Tony Alessandra, author of 13 books, veteran of over 2,000 paid speeches, taught several hundred people the easiest, most fun way to master people skills and selling skills. Now he wants to teach you too.

Yes. There have been countless books and videos produced on this subject, but if you weren't in Detroit, you have not seen the best of the best. And it was magic.

> *"If you have ever had a personality conflict*
> *with another human being - get this DVD."*

After you watch this DVD, you'll understand why corporations like IBM, Ford, AT&T and numerous other Fortune 500 companies are willing to pay Tony thousands of dollars for 60 minutes of his time.

But don't be fooled. Even though Tony keeps you laughing, he doesn't forget to deliver powerful content. Apply the simple techniques Tony shares with you and you get immediate results.

Dr. Tony has spent over 30 years tweaking his findings into two simple questions. Know the answers to these two questions, along with some additional knowledge Tony shares with in this highly entertaining DVD, and you hold the key to one of the most powerful human relationship concepts in the world. Don't put off getting this DVD of Dr. Tony in action. You'll watch it again and again.

BUY IT NOW! http://www.alessandra.com/products/productdetails. asp?productid=23

The Platinum Rule Video Training

How to train your team to have instant rapport and immediate chemistry with your customers, suppliers and each other.

> *"Whether you're selling, negotiating, or dealing*
> *with problem customers, knowing and applying*
> *The Platinum Rule will increase your success."*

Your people will get interested right from the start. Unlike many training films done in studio with "talking-heads" – this was filmed in front of a "live" audience of hundreds of people. Dr. Tony Alessandra shares his simple, fun and easy to understand techniques on how to deal with other people much more effectively.

It's fun. It's easy. It works!

Yes. There have been countless books, and videos produced on this subject – but if you haven't seen Dr. Tony, you have missed the best of the best. Tony's "from-the-streets-of-New York City style" is anything but boring. It's pure magic. But best of all, it's filled with immediately usable and effective content.

> *"If your employees have ever had a personality conflict with one of your customers – get this video training series."*

After your people experience this training – you'll understand why corporations like IBM, Ford, AT&T and numerous other Fortune 500 companies are willing to pay Tony thousands of dollars for only 60 minutes of his time.

This program is a comprehensive video-based training program that can be taught in either a half-day or full-day format. It includes a 48-minute video divided into several sections with lively lecturettes as well as entertaining vignettes by professional actors. It also includes a comprehensive 100+ page leader's guide with easy step-by-step instructions for facilitating the entire training program. Plus, it includes 10 extensive participant kits, each of which includes an invaluable assessment-package consisting of one self-evaluation, five observer evaluations, and a scoring matrix; a 63-page workbook, a 40-minute audio summary of the course, and a laminated pocket-sized summary card for reinforced learning.

But don't be fooled. Even though Tony keeps you laughing – he doesn't forget to deliver high caliber "customer-satisfying" content. It's simple. Apply the easy-to-understand and proven techniques Tony shares with you, and you get immediate results.

Buy It Now! http://www.alessandra.com/products/productdetails. asp?productid=24

Flexibility eWorkbook - *25-page PDF eWorkbook*

Do you respond to certain people, conditions, or events out of fear or anxiety? Are you unwilling to change your perspectives or positions in certain situations? Do you tend to face ambiguous situations negatively? If so, you may have predetermined views, conclusions, or patterns of behavior that are driving your actions - and impairing your flexibility. When you voluntarily refrain from participating in certain situations or interacting with certain people because of your lack of flexibility - therefore limiting your horizons - you decrease your chances of personal and professional success.

The Flexibility eWorkbook is an interactive tool for analyzing your personal attitudes toward yourself, others, and the situations you face. This workbook is a powerful tool that will help you dispel those attitudes that are holding you back from realizing your full potential.

TOPICS COVERED INCLUDE:

• Helping you increase your tolerance and respect for others, your confidence, and your positiveness - all of which enhance your flexibility

• Helping you decrease your rigidity, discontent, and competitive drive - all of which hinder your flexibility

BUY IT NOW! http://www.alessandra.com/products/productdetails. asp?productid=61

Versatility eWorkbook - *27-page PDF eWorkbook*

Are you stuck in a rut? Do you maintain the same routine way of doing things, regardless of changes in circumstances? If so, you may lack versatility - and you may be suffering the consequences as change passes you by.

The Versatility eWorkbook is an interactive tool for helping you dispel attitudes of low versatility that may have become deeply ingrained as a part of your basic personality. This workbook will help you change some of your habitual behaviors and knee-jerk reactions in order to become more versatile - and therefore increase your chances of success in any given situation, regardless of circumstances.

TOPICS COVERED INCLUDE:

- Helping you increase your resiliency, attentiveness, and vision - all of which enhance your versatility
- Helping you decrease your bluntness, resistance, and subjectiveness - all of which hinder your versatility

BUY IT NOW! http://www.alessandra.com/products/productdetails. asp?productid=60

Astounding Customer Service Complete Package

DVD - All eight chapters (segments) on Customer Service (approx. 80 minutes) PLUS three chapters on Listening Skills (approx. 36 minutes) PLUS two chapters on Telephone Skills (approx. 25 minutes), includes PDF Workbook for each category.

The cost of training your employees to deliver Astounding Customer Service never exceeds the cost of losing a customer!

Can you afford to lose your customers? Of course not, but you may be doing so anyway, if your company's customer service standards are not high enough for your customers. Luckily, employees in all areas of your business can easily and quickly increase their customer service skills - anyone from secretaries to managers to the CEO him/herself! Why not invest in my proven system today, and help your employees learn skills that will secure committed and active customers for your business? How can you afford not to?

CUSTOMER SERVICE TOPICS INCLUDE:

- Customer Service in America is Broken

- What's Your Customer Worth?

- Customer Service Demands Commitment, Communication, and Conflict Resolution

- Exceeding Customer Expectations

- The 3 R's of Customer Service

- How to Deliver Astounding Customer Service

- Graduate from One-Shot Sales to Lifetime Customers

- Improve Your Customer Service Language

LISTENING SKILLS TOPICS INCLUDE:
- The High Cost of Ineffective Listening

- The Benefits of Active Listening

- The CARESS Model

- Telephone Skills Topics Include:

- Sixteen Critical Strategies

- Handling Irate Callers

- Twelve Ideas Customers Love

- My personal guarantee!

If you're not satisfied with the results I'm positive you'll see in the first 60 days, pick up the phone or send me an email and I'll refund your money on the spot! No questions asked. How's that for customer service?

BUY IT NOW! http://www.alessandra.com/products/productdetails.asp?productid=66

Printed in the United States
120111LV00011B/193-213/A

9 781933 596617